Worship through the Seasons

Reflective Services for the Christian Year

Nick Fawcett

kevin mayhew

kevin
mayhew

First published in Great Britain in 2011 by Kevin Mayhew Ltd
Buxhall, Stowmarket, Suffolk IP14 3BW
Tel: +44 (0) 1449 737978 Fax: +44 (0) 1449 737834
E-mail: info@kevinmayhewltd.com

www.kevinmayhew.com

9 8 7 6 5 4 3 2 1 0

ISBN 978 1 84867 390 8
Catalogue No. 1501283

Cover design by Rob Mortonson

Project managed by Free Range Book Design & Production

Printed and bound in Great Britain

Contents

Foreword

Few issues in the Church today are more contentious than worship. Its importance, in the minds of many, far outweighs theological, doctrinal or denominational differences. For some, the very idea of straying from tried and trusted patterns is tantamount to heresy. For others, those patterns have become associated with lifeless formality and, in consequence, have been abandoned. Personally, I believe we must make room for both viewpoints, respecting and building on tradition but at the same time being open to new ideas. One such idea I experimented with during my ministry was using meditations, music and slides to bring out the meaning of Scripture. My aim was to engage the senses in a way that would capture the imagination of those participating in worship, breathing fresh life into old and familiar passages, and offering insight into the not-so-familiar. In time, the various meditations I wrote for such services found their way into print in two of my early books, *No Ordinary Man* books 1 and 2, the reflective service outlines from which were subsequently published in a series of books under the general title *Worship through the seasons*.

Here, now, is an addition to that series, drawn from the three volumes of my recent worship resource *A most amazing man*. It brings together, in one book, service outlines for each of the major seasons of the Christian year: Advent, Christmas, Epiphany, Lent, the opening days of Holy Week, Maundy Thursday, Good Friday, and Easter. Each comes complete with introductions, link comments, meditations and prayers, together with suggestions for hymns, biblical readings and audiovisual resources – you will need only to add intercessions.

Whether you decide to use the suggested audiovisual material is up to you; omitting slides and/or music makes for a more traditional service that is undoubtedly easier to stage, but you will lose the impact made through engaging the wider senses. Many of the slide collections (see the Appendix) are very hard to get hold of today but, with ever-changing technology and corresponding resource material being produced, you may be able to find – via an online search – the same or similar material in PowerPoint format. If you do make use of slides, you will need to go through the suggested material carefully and select that which most effectively complements each reading and meditation. You may, instead, decide to use just the suggested music, which in each case has been carefully chosen with the reading and meditation in mind. An effective way of presenting the music is to fade the volume after an interval so that the relevant Scripture passage can be read over it, before bringing back up the volume again and continuing to the end of the piece (or, if the piece is a long one, to when you decide to fade out the music completely).

When using audiovisual material, there are obviously certain basic requirements. A good hi-fi system, slide projector and screen are essential, as is an effective amplification system so that readers' voices carry over any background music. You will also find the services of an assistant invaluable when it comes to presenting the material – ideally somebody to control the slide projector, and possibly someone to fade the music in and out as appropriate. Always run through slides beforehand, making sure they are the right way up and in the correct order. Make sure also that you have a spare bulb in case one should blow, and arrange all electrical leads so that no one can inadvertently fall over them. The less you leave to chance, the less possibility there will be of anything going wrong. Remember, also, to ensure that those reading the meditations are given proper time to prepare beforehand, and that they are instructed to read slowly and clearly, beginning by announcing the title of the meditation.

You can probably borrow much of the recommended music from your local library or a friend. Should you prefer to buy it, much is available on budget CD sets. I made particular use of *The Voices of Angels (100 Heavenly Classics), 100 Romantic Classics, 100 Relaxing Classics* and *100 Popular Classics,* (Castle Communications); *Discovering the Classics* (three volume double CD set), *Renaissance Choral Treasures* and *Classical Favourites for Relaxing and Dreaming* (Naxos; the *Classic Experience* discs 1 and 3 (EMI); and Classic FM's *All Time Christmas Greats*. Other works extensively used are Handel's *Messiah*, Mozart's *Requiem*, *Mass in C minor* and *Coronation Mass*, and the various compositions of Margaret Rizza and Keith Duke, available from Kevin Mayhew Publishers.

Organising a service of this kind undeniably takes time and effort but, in my experience, this is well worth putting in. It is a very different style of worship from what most people will be used to, but perhaps because of this it may be able to bridge the gap between diverse contemporary patterns and understandings of worship, and, more importantly, speak to those who may not usually contemplate attending church. If this book helps to achieve that then it will more than justify the hours I have spent in putting it together.

Nick Fawcett

About the author

Nick Fawcett trained for the Baptist ministry at Bristol and Oxford, before going on to serve in pastorates in Leigh, Lancashire, and Gas Green, Cheltenham. He subsequently spent three years as a chaplain with the Christian movement Toc H, before deciding the time was right to commit himself to a writing ministry, supplementing his income through freelance editing. He has written over a hundred and twenty books, many of which have sold thousands of copies.

Together with their two children, Samuel and Kate, he lives with his wife, Deborah, in Wellington, Somerset, worshipping at the local Anglican church. A keen walker, gardener and chess player, as well as supporter of Southend United and local team Tiverton Town, Nick delights in the beauty of the Somerset and Devon countryside around his home, his numerous books owing much to the inspiration he unfailingly finds there.

Advent

Advent (1)

Suggested visual material

Jesus of Nazareth 1
Jesus of Nazareth 2
The Life of Christ I
The Life of Christ II

Introduction

'Be prepared,' says the Boy Scouts' motto, and that, in a nutshell, is also the message at the heart of Advent. But be prepared for what? Despite what the hustle and bustle associated with this time of year may tell you, these few weeks are not just about getting ready for Christmas – writing cards, buying presents, stocking up with food, hanging decorations and so forth. Rather, they are about ensuring we're ready to meet Jesus should he come again, to honour him in our hearts and serve him with our lives, to hear his call and glimpse his presence in the world around us. Whoever we are, none of us are as ready as we like to think. Advent offers us the opportunity to take stock, to reflect, and to respond.

Opening prayer

Redeemer God,
prepare us to worship you:
to recognise your love, mercy, purpose and power
and to offer our heartfelt praise.
Prepare us to serve you:
to understand your will and respond to your calling,
consecrating our lives to the growth of your kingdom
in thought, word and deed.
Prepare us to know you:
to learn more of your goodness, truth and nature,
your work in human history across the years.
Prepare us to welcome you:
to live each day,
each moment,
in the light of your promises,
ready to welcome our saviour Christ
when he comes again in glory.
Make straight a highway in the wilderness of our lives,

so that he may work in and through us,
by your grace.
Amen.

Hymn The light of the morning is breaking

Comment A watched kettle, they say, never boils, which of course is another way of saying that the more we look forward to something the longer it seems to take in coming. The lesson is simple: don't waste your time counting down the minutes, days, weeks or months before the anticipated event happens. Get on with the day-to-day business of living, assured that the day you are waiting for will come in its own good time. If that's true of little things – birthdays or holidays, for example – it's true all the more of the expectation at the heart of Advent: the promised return of Christ. Should we look forward to that? Yes. Should it dominate our thinking? No. Or at least not in the sense of dwelling and speculating on end times. The whys and wherefores of his coming are not for us to know. We are called simply to trust that the day will dawn and to prepare for it by serving him in our daily lives, here and now.

Music *Come, Lord (Music for Advent and Christmas)*
Margaret Rizza

Reading Matthew 24:36–44

Meditation of Thomas
'How long will it be?' we asked him.
'How long before the end of the age,
the dawn of his kingdom,
when wrongs will be righted
and good triumph over evil?'
We wanted answers,
the time and place spelt out,
so that we'd know where we stood
and could plan ahead accordingly.
Yet he not only *wouldn't* say –
he *couldn't,*
for he didn't have the answer himself.
That seemed strange at first,

but it shouldn't have,
for it made us trust in the Father
just as he did.
And if we *had* known,
if we could have pinned down the time of his coming –
ten, fifty, a hundred years –
what would have been our response?
Would devotion have faded,
only to return as the day drew near?
Would we have lived for the present
until the future was upon us?
Who can say?
But ultimately it was the wrong question –
for the kingdom starts now,
growing within,
to be lived as much as proclaimed,
celebrated today as well as expected tomorrow.
Lose sight of that and, however ready we may feel,
we'll never be prepared for his coming.

Silence

Prayer Eternal God,
help us to know you now,
love you now,
serve you now –
to live each day as your people,
seeking and honouring your will.
Open our hearts to the reality
of your kingdom among us
and teach us more of your way,
so that in everything we do, think and say
we may work to help it grow,
bringing your purpose to fruition.
Learning from all you have done and will yet do,
help us to trust you in the present,
consecrating each moment in faithful discipleship,
to the glory of your name.
Amen.

Hymn God is working his purpose out

Comment 'Prepare in the wilderness the way of the Lord' – that's what John the Baptist, above all others, is celebrated for having done: preaching, teaching and baptising in the wilderness to make ready the way of Christ. But he spoke also of *us* getting ready, asking one question in particular: how ready are we to change? Responding to Christ means turning from our old way of life to a new, aligning ourselves with his will and seeking to follow where he leads, acknowledging our faults and seeking new beginnings. And that's not just a one-off response. It's one we need to go on making day after day, for though we seek to serve, we fail; though we strive to be different, we so often stay the same. We can't change ourselves, but Advent speaks of the transformation made possible in Christ. As our next reading and meditation remind us, it calls us to ask what still needs changing in our lives and to open our hearts afresh to God's renewing touch.

Music *Kyrie eleison (Messe de Minuit)* Charpentier

Reading Matthew 3:1–12

Meditation of a listener to John the Baptist

'Repent,' he told us;
'bear fruit worthy of repentance.'
But what did he mean?
A prophet, some called him,
but I wasn't so sure –
for with his camel-hair clothes,
desert lifestyle
and diet of locusts and honey
he came across as eccentric rather than inspired,
a tub-thumping fanatic rather than man of God.
'You brood of vipers!' he called us;
'worthless chaff!'
What had we done, for him to turn on us like that?
Of what shocking sins did we stand accused?
It was only later that I understood,
after I'd heard and seen the one he pointed to,
listened to Jesus of Nazareth

and witnessed the way he lived,
loved,
died and rose again.
He turned our faith on its head, Jesus –
rewrote religion,
gave the Scriptures a whole new meaning –
for he showed us a different way,
unlike any we'd seen before:
the way of love, compassion and forgiveness,
of others first and self second,
of awesome grace and truth.
That's what John was on about there in the wilderness.
He was calling us to a change of direction,
a turning from one life to another,
for though he spoke of sin and repentance,
he was heralding the one who,
far from holding our faults against us,
would bear them all on the cross;
the one who came not to condemn but to pardon,
to make us and all things new.

Silence

Prayer Gracious God,
thank you for your generous love
and awesome mercy –
your willingness to welcome us back
when we go astray,
to time and again pardon our sins.
Remind us of what it cost you to make that possible:
of the awesome truth that, through your Son,
you not only shared our life
but also endured our death,
atoning on the cross for our sin.
Teach us, then, to be truly sorry,
and, in heartfelt gratitude,
to turn from our old ways to embrace the new.
Direct our path,
and put a right spirit within us,
so that our lives may bear fruit for you.
Amen.

Hymn Of the Father's love begotten

Comment John the Baptist began his ministry full of hope and anticipation but, as time passed, all that was to change, his preaching incurring the fury of Herod, who had him carted off to prison. Understandably, his languishing there caused John to question, to wonder if God was at work in Christ after all. We too, when we look at our world – its sorrow and suffering, evil and injustice – can feel the same. Is the gospel really good news or simply wishful thinking? As we shall see, for John the answer came in reports of what Jesus was doing: changing lives, making a difference to so many people in so many ways. And, despite everything that is wrong in our world, that goes on being true across the centuries, God's Spirit working in countless ways to bring new life, new beginnings. Advent asks if we're ready to keep faith even when life is hard; whether the commitment we professed yesterday is still as real today.

Music *Come, my Lord, my light, my way (Sacred Weave)*
Keith Duke

Reading Matthew 11:2–11

Meditation of John the Baptist

'Are you the one,' I asked –
'the one we've been waiting for,
yearning for,
across the centuries?'
I should have known, you say,
without need of confirmation,
but remember,
I'd been locked up in prison for months
with no news of anything or anyone,
and it was hard to understand
why God had let that happen,
let alone to keep faith in the future.
What if I'd been wrong,
mistaken the signs?
What if the man I'd baptised
wasn't the Messiah after all,

the chosen one of God?
It could all have been some ghastly mistake,
and, in my dark, dank cell,
that thought had begun to haunt me.
So when word filtered through
that Jesus was at work,
his words creating a stir,
naturally I wanted to know more,
to gauge whether my first impressions had been right
and not some deluded dream.
I sent out my followers to learn more,
and the news they brought me said it all –
of the blind able to see,
the lame to walk,
lepers made whole
and the dead raised;
of good news for the poor,
justice for the weak
and hope for the oppressed –
ancient promises fulfilled at last.
I remain a captive of course,
I'd expected that,
but I'm free nonetheless,
for the one I'd longed to see had come at last,
bringing liberty to all.
I'd lived to see the dawn of his kingdom.
Now, if necessary, I was ready to die for it, too.

Silence

Prayer Loving God,
for the countless ways
you've transformed people's lives,
restoring and renewing,
we praise you.
For giving strength to the weak,
hope to the oppressed,
freedom to those held captive
and healing to the sick,
we worship you.
For bringing joy to the sorrowful,
peace to the troubled,

and light to those in darkness,
we thank you.
And, above all,
for conquering evil with good,
hatred with love
and death with life,
we honour and acclaim you.
Humbly and gratefully,
we offer our lives to your service
and for the work of your kingdom.
Amen.

Hymn A great and mighty wonder

Comment For Zechariah and Elizabeth, the birth of their son John was something special, amazing, an act of God. Yet the words for which Zechariah is most celebrated marvel not at the gift of their boy but at the one whom that child would proclaim and whose way he would prepare. The true miracle lay in Jesus, his birth being an event to shout about from the rooftops, to exult in, to give thanks for from the bottom of one's heart, for here was one who would change the world, bringing light, love and hope into the barrenness of human lives. Have we captured that sense of joy and thankfulness? And, more important, do we continue to feel it? Advent calls us to prepare once again to worship and welcome the King of kings, and Lord of lords – God's awesome gift in Christ.

Music *O magnum mysterium (Music for Advent and Christmas)*
Margaret Rizza

Reading Luke 1:67–79

Meditation of Zechariah, father of John the Baptist

I knew it was the start of something big,
not just for the two of us,
but for everyone,
the whole world –
this child we were promised
destined to point beyond himself
to one greater,
sent by God to bring life, hope and redemption to all.
Our boy would be the herald,
born to prepare the way,
to make straight in the desert a highway for our God.
But if *he* was the supporting cast,
the star would swiftly follow:
the dayspring from on high.
John would speak of sin . . .
Jesus of pardon;
John of repentance . . .
Jesus of new life –
one identifying the root of our problems,
the other offering the answers we seek.
It was the start of something special –
for me and Elizabeth,
for Joseph and Mary,
for everyone, everywhere,
past, present and future –
but quite *how* special I'd barely begun to grasp.
How about *you*?

Silence

Prayer

Forgive us, Lord,
for we struggle to grasp the wonder of your love,
the miracle of what you have done in Christ.
We lose sight of the reality
that you lived and died among us,
walking our earth,
sharing our humanity.
We forget that the stable at Bethlehem
was the start of something
that would change history for ever,
its impact still reverberating around the world today.

We fail to understand
the way you can work in our lives,
with small beginnings bringing unexpected results
out of all proportion to our faith.
Speak again now of all you have *done,*
are doing
and *will do,*
and help us to celebrate with body, mind and soul
the priceless blessing of your gift in Christ.
Amen.

Hymn Earth was waiting, spent and restless

Closing prayer Lord Jesus Christ,
be born in us.
speak to us,
work through us,
shine from us.
Take our hands,
our feet,
our lips,
our lives
and use them to your glory.
Forgive our faults,
renew our faith,
restore our vision,
receive our service.
Come among us
and work your miracle of grace within our hearts,
so that we may honour you now
and be ready to welcome you when you come again.
Amen.

Advent (2)

Suggested visual material

Jesus of Nazareth 1
Jesus of Nazareth 2
The Life of Christ I
The Life of Christ II

Introduction

Compared to Christmas, Advent tends to be the poor relation, dutifully remembered but its relevance passing many by. For those outside the Church its four weeks are little more than the last chance to complete their Christmas shopping and other festive preparations, and even many Christians see it as essentially a prelude to their Yuletide celebrations. But Advent is much more. It's an invitation to look again at the bigger picture of the gospel, from the announcement of Christ's coming to his coming again. It's an opportunity to examine ourselves, asking whether we'd be happy to meet with Christ should he return here and now. And, most of all, it's a reminder of the gracious purpose of God, unfolding across history, to enfold all in his saving love. As we listen today to the words of Scripture and reflections upon their message, use them to prepare yourself not just for Advent, but for life itself, lived with him – now and eternally.

Opening prayer

Living God,
speak again in this Advent season
of your redeeming love,
your desire to forgive, restore and renew.
Speak of the unfolding of your purpose
through Law and prophets,
gloriously fulfilled in the birth of your Son
and his living, dying and resurrection.
Speak of his coming again to establish your kingdom,
to rule on earth and in heaven,
and to raise us to newness of life
lived for ever with you.
Prepare our hearts to listen,
to learn,

to reflect,
to respond,
and so may this time draw us closer to you,
by his grace deepening our faith
and strengthening our commitment.
Amen.

Hymn Lord Jesus, at your coming

Comment For Luke the gospel story starts with not just one announcement of a child to be born, but two. Before Mary learns that she's to bear the Christ child, Zechariah is told that his wife Elizabeth is to bear a son, who will prepare the saviour's way. As we heard in that reading, he was amazed, incredulous, unable at first to take it in, and little wonder. So what would he have made of the experience, looking back? What did he see as the significance of his son's birth? And, most of all, what did it teach him about God? It's questions such as these that we'll explore in our first reading and meditation.

Music *Il riposo – per il Santissimo Natale (Concerto for strings)* Vivaldi

Reading Luke 1:67–79

Meditation of Zechariah, father of John the Baptist

Are you afraid of God?
We were.
Oh yes, we called him good, compassionate, faithful,
slow to anger and full of love,
yet above all he was a God out there –
mighty,
sovereign,
omnipotent –
and we were afraid to get too close
for fear of the consequences.
Put a foot wrong, we reasoned,
and he would strike us down,
descend on us like a ton of bricks,
for he was holy and righteous,
quick to punish as well as bless –

a jealous and vengeful God
more likely to judge than pardon our mistakes.
We don't think that now though,
not any more,
for my son, John, was to usher in a new era,
preparing the way of the Lord.
Do you wonder I felt so excited!
No longer would God be remote,
detached.
He was coming among us,
entering our world to make possible a relationship
that we could never establish ourselves.
It would change everything –
our faith,
our lives,
our world.
No more trembling before God.
No more approaching him with dread.
Reverence, certainly,
but also trust,
confidence,
gratitude
and joy.
The day of the Lord was upon us,
the dawn of his kingdom.
Just as he had promised,
we would worship him on high,
yet know him by our side;
acclaim him in awe,
yet serve without fear.

Silence

Prayer Sovereign God,
give us a proper sense of awe before you,
of reverence, respect and humility.
Remind us that you are the beginning and end of all,
the creator of the ends of the earth
and giver of life and meaning.
But help us to remember also that you took flesh,
coming among us in Christ
and identifying yourself with humankind,

and that you did so not to condemn and punish
but to express the immensity of your love.
Gratefully, we celebrate your grace,
through which we worship and serve you,
assured of your unfailing goodness and mercy.
Amen.

Hymn Tell out, my soul

Comment There aren't many people who, simply by speaking, can command an audience, but John the Baptist was clearly one of them, so much so that crowds not only gathered to hear him but actively sought him out in the wilderness, intent on hearing his message. And, perhaps unsurprisingly, it wasn't long before rumours started to circulate that he was the promised Messiah, the one for whom the Jewish nation had waited for so long. How must John have felt about that? Happy? Encouraged? Proud? You'd imagine so. But if his preaching and teaching was so successful, why then was he only a bit part, the forerunner sent to prepare the way of the Lord, whom he was called to baptise? Would you, in John's shoes, have been tempted to ask that question? Did he ever resent the role assigned to him? It would have been a natural enough human response, yet if anyone was determined to avoid any possible misunderstanding as to who he was and what he'd come to do, it was surely John. As our next reading and meditation explore however, it's harder than we may think not to give the wrong impression.

Music *And the glory of the Lord (Messiah)* Handel

Reading John 1:6–8, 19–28

Meditation of John the Baptist

Who was I, they wanted to know,
and I knew full well what they were thinking:
that I was the Messiah,
the promised one of God,
come at last to set them free.
Why wouldn't they listen!
I'd spent weeks, months, out there in the wilderness,

pointing to the Christ,
preparing his way,
and yet it all seemed to be in vain.
Clearly I had to spell things out –
so that's what I did.
'Let's get this straight,' I said, 'once and for all:
it's not me!'
But still they kept on,
their minds, it seems, already made up.
I could have knocked their heads together,
such was my frustration,
but the misunderstanding wasn't entirely their fault,
much though I wish it were.
Somehow, despite my best intentions,
I'd put across too much of *me*
and too little of *him*.
Perhaps it was the camel-hair clothes,
the diet of locusts and honey,
the desert lifestyle –
who can say? –
but, whatever it was,
I'd obviously sent out mixed messages,
failing to point as unmistakably to Christ as I imagined.
What about you?
Do you make the same mistake?
You may not think so,
but, take it from me, it's easily done,
what you say and do
and what you *think* you say and do
not necessarily the same.
So ask yourself this, prayerfully and honestly:
who does your life speak of –
you or Jesus?
The answer may surprise you,
as it did me.

Silence

Prayer Remind us, Lord, that we are called to witness
not to ourselves,
the Bible
or the Church,
but to you:
to what you said,
what you have done
and who you are.
Forgive us for losing sight of that,
unconsciously putting across a different message.
Forgive us for confusing incidentals
with what really matters.
Help us to seek your glory before our own,
putting you first and self second,
so that, in all we do,
we may truly honour your name.
Amen.

Hymn Hail to the Lord's anointed

Comment John's Gospel offers one perspective on the ministry of John the Baptist; Mark gives another, his account being a more straightforward description of John's preaching and baptising in the wilderness. He explicitly portrays John as fulfilling the words of the prophet Isaiah: 'See, I am sending my messenger ahead of you, who will prepare your way; the voice of one crying out in the wilderness: "Prepare the way of the Lord, make his paths straight."' That is what John understood himself to be; how he would have summarised his role. And if he could speak to us today, that would be the burden of his message: are we as ready as we like to think we are to welcome Christ when he comes? Should he appear today, would you be prepared to meet him?

Music *O come, O come, Immanuel (Advent carol)*

Reading Mark 1:1–8

Meditation of John the Baptist

You've heard of the Romans I suppose?
A decadent lot, to put it mildly –
but I'll say this for them:
they know how to build roads.
There are dozens everywhere,
even out here in the wilderness,
running straight and true, mile after mile,
and what a difference they've made,
journeys that once took a week
now being a matter of days.
Not that Rome cares about us, of course.
They're thinking only of their armies.
One sniff of trouble,
let alone rebellion,
and they can be down on us now like a ton of bricks,
legions hurried in from across the world.
But you've got to admire their foresight –
how they're prepared, it seems, for anything.
I'm following their example, in a sense,
creating a road of a different sort,
into the wilderness of human lives,
for my task is to prepare the way of the Lord,
to make straight a path for his coming.
He'll be here soon, you see,
the day being almost upon us,
but will you be ready receive him –
ready to hear his voice and meet his gaze,
to answer when he calls?
Oh, you may think so,
but don't be fooled,
for most of those who've come out to me
here in the wilderness
aren't even close.
So take heed,
listen to my words,
and be prepared,
so that, whenever he comes, he may find the road clear,
a highway into your heart.

Silence

Prayer Lord Jesus Christ,
prepare a way in our hearts
so that you may more fully enter in.
Break down the barriers of doubt and disbelief
that keep us from you –
the faults and failings that deny your love
and obstruct your purpose.
Fill us with your love,
redeem us by your grace
and renew us by your power,
Make your path straight within us,
so that, consecrated to your service,
we, in turn, may help to prepare your way
in the lives of others.
Amen.

Hymn Make way, make way

Comment If Advent looks back to the first coming of Jesus and the call of John the Baptist to prepare his way, it also looks forward to his coming again and our need to be ready to greet him then. When will that be? Where? How will it happen? What will it involve? In the Gospels, Jesus gives solemn warnings of troubled times prior to his return, calling his followers to be ready yet urging them not to dwell on the date and time but to leave such details in the hands of God. Many across the years have done the opposite, confidently predicting the end, just as many in the early church were convinced that the last days were upon them. Imagine yourself as one of the latter. What would you have made of Jesus' words? And in what way would hope for the future have shaped your experience of the present?

Music *Dies irae (Requiem)* Mozart

Reading Mark 13:24–37

Meditation of a modern-day Christian

The sun dark,
moon dull,
stars falling from heaven?
Well if that's happened, *I* haven't heard,
nor anyone else, come to that.
There's been the odd eclipse, of course,
meteors too,
but nothing to worry about –
no upheaval to shatter the cosmos
and signal the end of time.
So what did Jesus mean,
claiming his own generation would see such things?
Was he wrong,
deluded,
or could he have meant something else?
Do you know what: I think he did,
for he talked of *heaven and earth* passing away,
not *us* –
of his elect being gathered together
when these things happen,
to welcome him on his return.
This life may end, in other words,
but not the life to come,
our hope being in things unseen –
a kingdom beyond this world.
That's what matters:
faith in the future shaping the present,
so that instead of fretting about what lies ahead
we live now as he would wish.
I'm not saying it won't happen,
the end of life as we know it –
no doubt one day it will –
but his point was we have nothing to fear,
for he will be with us always,
faithful though all else may fail.
Don't brood on tomorrow.
Rejoice today,
and trust in him.
We may pass *on* before he comes,
but we will never pass *away*.

Silence

Prayer Almighty God,
thank you for giving us joy in the present
and hope for the future;
the sure and certain knowledge
that your love not only surrounds us now,
but will continue to do so for all eternity,
nothing in heaven or earth,
life or death,
being able to separate us from it.
Deepen our faith in everything you hold in store,
and may that assurance shape every aspect
of who and what we are.
Teach us to trust, serve and live for you,
today and always.
Amen.

Hymn Lo, he comes with clouds descending

Closing prayer Lord Jesus Christ,
promised of old,
foretold by prophets,
long awaited by your people,
we worship you.
Saviour Christ,
rejected and despised,
nailed to a cross and sealed in a tomb,
we acclaim you.
Risen Christ,
here through your Spirit,
here by our sides,
we welcome you.
Sovereign Christ,
coming to redeem your people,
to reign in glory
and to welcome us into your kingdom,
we thank you.
Make us ready, this and every day,
to greet you when you come,
and to live each moment
rejoicing in the light of your love.
Amen.

Advent (3)

Suggested visual material

Jesus of Nazareth 1
Jesus of Nazareth 2
The Life of Christ I
The Life of Christ II

Introduction

We are here in the season of Advent – the first season of the Christian year and beginning of the Christian calendar. But what is this time all about? Is it simply, as some tend to see it, part of the build-up to Christmas – a rehearsal, as it were, for the great celebration of our saviour's birth? No. It's far more than that, speaking of both endings and new beginnings, of judgement yet forgiveness, of expectation and being prepared. It calls us, as we make ready to celebrate the coming of Jesus into the world, to reflect on the Christ who is beyond and who, in the fullness of time, will come again to establish his kingdom. Through prayers, hymns, readings and meditations, let us reflect now on what that means: for us and for all.

Opening prayer

Loving God,
we want to worship you:
prepare our hearts;
we want to know you better:
prepare our minds;
we want to serve you:
prepare our lives.
For your coming to us in Christ,
bringing love, joy, peace and new beginnings,
receive our praise.
For your promise that he will come again,
establishing your kingdom and fulfilling your will,
accept our thanks.
For our failure to honour him as we should,
our weak commitment and half-hearted discipleship,
grant your pardon.
For our world of pain and need,
sorrow and suffering

hear our prayer.
Meet with us now,
speak your word,
and in the wilderness of our lives,
make straight a highway for the Lord to come.
Amen.

Hymn O come, O come, Emmanuel

Comment If Jesus lies at the heart of Advent, then one of the foremost among the supporting cast is surely John the Baptist, the one sent by God to prepare his way. John's call to repentance was to find glorious fulfilment in Christ's gift of forgiveness and new beginnings. But let's go back to another beginning: the promise of John's birth, so powerfully captured in the words of Luke.

Music *Christus natus est (Fire of Love)* Margaret Rizza

Reading Luke 1:67–79

Meditation of Zechariah, father of John the Baptist

Overwrought, some said I was,
the trauma of being struck dumb for all those months
finally taking its toll.
Others said it was excitement talking,
the joy of seeing our child,
my own flesh and blood,
lying there before us –
our prayers answered after so many disappointments.
A few didn't know what to think,
unsure whether I'd had one too many
or taken leave of my senses,
but whatever it was, I just couldn't help myself,
the words bubbling up within me and gushing out,
unstoppable,
a spontaneous outpouring of praise,
a torrent of thanksgiving.
And no, it wasn't just about *my* child,
despite what some might think,
but also, and above all,
about the one he was destined to serve:

a child like none other
who would answer *all* our prayers
in a way too wonderful for words!
If John brought new beginnings for Elizabeth and I,
this child would bring something far more wonderful:
a fresh start for everyone,
a clean slate,
new hope, joy, peace and life.
Of course I didn't know the full story then,
not even the half of it,
but God had revealed enough to stir my spirit,
setting my heart racing and pulse tingling,
for the saviour was coming,
the promised deliverer,
bringing salvation,
forgiveness,
light from on high –
a relationship with God
deeper than anything we'd dreamt possible.
Like I say, it seemed too wonderful for words,
but then that picture struck me,
of a new dawn,
sunshine scattering the darkness,
a fresh start full of untold possibilities,
and that, succinctly yet eloquently, seemed to say it all.
The night was nearly over,
day about to break.
At last the sun was rising,
never again to set.

Silence

Prayer Come, Lord, into the darkness of our world,
the shadow of sorrow,
suffering,
hunger,
despair,
hatred,
evil
and death.

Bring a new dawn,
new beginnings,
the light of your love shining on all.
Amen.

Hymn The angel Gabriel from heaven came

Comment If John the Baptist is integral to the season of Advent, one other is more important still, second only to Jesus in significance. I speak, of course, of Mary, whose faith, courage and commitment has inspired generations across the centuries. Nowhere more so do those qualities shine out than in her response to the visitation of Gabriel and the call to bear God's son.

Music *Ave Maria* Cuccini (arr. Prizeman)

Reading Luke 1:39–55

Meditation of Mary, mother of Jesus

They'll call me blessed,
most favoured among women,
and I can understand why,
for incredibly God has chosen *me* to bear his son,
me to carry the promised Messiah in my womb.
It's an honour beyond words,
a privilege no one could ever earn or deserve,
least of all me,
and I don't mind admitting
that I'm still reeling with the wonder of it all.
Yes, it will involve wagging tongues,
knowing winks,
disapproving glances –
and no doubt Joseph will have a thing or two
to say about it as well –
but however awkward or painful that may be,
it is more than worth it for the joy of being chosen
and of offering myself in the service of the Lord.
Yet don't think I'm the only one blessed –
that this awesome earth-changing birth
concerns simply me
and not others –
for if you imagine that, you couldn't be more wrong.

It's good news for all of us,
every man, woman and child:
news that will transform our lives,
our history,
the world itself.
For this child is sent by God to redeem his people:
to bring freedom, hope, joy and peace,
deliverance from whatever holds us captive,
and forgiveness for all our sins.
Think about what that means:
new life,
new beginnings –
an end to sorrow and suffering,
darkness and despair,
to death itself.
It's what we've longed to see and so long waited for,
the answer to our prayers.
So yes, they'll call me blessed,
but never forget that the blessing is equally yours –
God's gracious gift being for me,
for you,
for everyone.
My soul magnifies the Lord
and rejoices in God my saviour!

Silence

Prayer

Lord Jesus Christ,
for your coming among us,
your gift of life,
and the peace, joy, hope and love you offer to all,
we worship you.
We praise you that you are still good news,
glad tidings not just for others
but for *us*.
With heart and soul,
all that we are,
together, we acclaim you.
Amen.

Hymn On Jordan's bank the Baptist's cry

Comment We return again now to John the Baptist, but this time moving on to his desert ministry. His preaching there focused on two key Advent themes: the faithful fulfilment of God's promises of old, and the challenge to prepare a way in our hearts for Christ's coming. As the following reading and meditation explore, that is not something we are left struggling to do alone.

Music *Every valley shall be exalted (Messiah)* Handel

Reading Luke 3:1–6

Meditation of a listener to John the Baptist

The words were familiar –
the prophet Isaiah's, I think –
speaking of the one to come,
a highway for our God.
But what did they actually mean?
Was there to be a new road through the wilderness,
some project of the Romans, perhaps,
which, by a strange twist of fate,
would allow the Messiah to march into Jerusalem
and drive them out?
It was a pleasant thought,
but somehow it didn't ring true,
for I knew of no such recent construction work,
yet John clearly believed the day of the Lord
was not just approaching,
but already here,
the kingdom dawning among us.
I was puzzled,
mystified,
until he pointed me to Jesus,
and then,
slowly,
all became clear,
for I saw the weak restored,
the broken healed,
the lost found,
the dead raised,
and gradually all that talk of valleys being filled in,

hills brought low,
the crooked made straight
and the rough becoming smooth
began to make sense.
It was happening all around me,
God treading a path
into the wilderness of human hearts:
empty souls being made full,
obstacles overcome,
lives transformed for ever.
In the coming of Christ,
new beginnings were possible,
not just for the few or in the here and now,
but for all flesh,
in every place and time:
you, me and everyone.
God had come among us,
sweeping aside whatever blocked his way
The desert has started to bloom.

Silence

Prayer Thank you, Lord, for what you have done,
what you are doing
and what you yet shall do.
Thank you that you not only came among us
but are with us now,
constantly at work through your Spirit
to bless, strengthen, guide and call.
Continue to perform in our hearts the miracle of grace,
so that we may know and love you better,
our lives speaking to all
of your saving and transforming love.
Amen.

Hymn Hark the glad sound! the Saviour comes

Comment We've focused twice already on John the Baptist, such is his centrality to Advent, yet – important though he was and is – he was never under any illusions about his significance in relation to Jesus. He was the forerunner, not the Messiah; a herald rather than the one heralded. In John's courageous witness to Christ, and his unassuming pointing away from himself and towards Jesus, are enduring lessons that once again take us to the heart of this season and its meaning for you and me today.

Music *And the glory of the Lord (Messiah)* Handel

Reading Luke 3:7–18

Meditation of John the Baptist

It wasn't just annoying, that talk of me as the Messiah,
it was embarrassing,
ridiculous,
even, to my mind, blasphemy.
You think I'm exaggerating?
Then think again,
for we couldn't have been more different, Jesus and I,
the two of us chalk and cheese,
a gaping chasm dividing us.
Yes, I immersed in water,
but he baptised with the Spirit,
and do you understand the distinction,
the importance of what that means?
While I offered a *symbol*,
a sign of repentance and desire to change,
he brought the real thing:
forgiveness,
new life,
the chance to be born again.
In a ministry I could only dream of,
he made the word flesh,
bestowing God's power and imparting his love in human hearts,
transforming from within.
So don't compare us,
still less confuse me with him,
for I'm unworthy even to tie his shoes.

I may have preached the kingdom of God,
even in some small way contributed towards it,
but he brought it among us
and will bring it to fulfilment –
so, you see,
there's literally all the difference in the world!

Silence

Prayer Lord Jesus Christ,
we have no claim on your goodness,
no right to expect your blessing,
for, compared to you, we are nothing –
weak,
stubborn,
foolish.
Yet you invite us not just to know you
but to make you known,
not just to love you
but to be loved in turn,
not just to enter your kingdom
but to help build it now.
Thank you for that awesome grace,
so undeserved
yet so freely given.
Amen.

Hymn Come, thou long-expected Jesus

Comment No Advent service is complete without reference to the dawn of God's kingdom and Christ's coming again. If the message of this season had to be reduced to one word then it would surely be this: 'expectation'. We look forward to a time when God's will is done, to a world where sorrow and suffering are at an end. But what does that mean for us here and now? Is our hope solely in the future, or do what we believe and who we believe in shape the present. In our final reading and meditation, we reflect on sobering words from the Gospel of Luke, asking how a member of the early church might have understood them and how we might make sense of them today.

Music But *who may abide the day of his coming? (Messiah)* Handel

Reading Luke 21:25–36

Meditation of a Christian in the early Church

What was he saying?
That we should welcome times of trouble?
Delight in adversity?
Even court disaster?
That distress and confusion are to be greeted with joy as signs of his coming?
I've heard some say so,
speculating at every catastrophe,
every crisis,
that the time is near,
his return surely upon us.
But days have come . . .
and days have gone . . .
with no sign that things will change.
Does that disturb me, you ask?
Not at all,
for to me his point was different:
about the present rather than future,
life on earth instead of life in heaven.
Our redemption *is* growing near,
of that I'm sure,
the fulfilment of God's purpose
little by little drawing closer,
but the time and details are not for us to know.
It *may* be in my lifetime,
it may not,
but what I will see for sure,
as *all* will see,
is war and rumours of war,
a world divided by hatred, suspicion and division,
suffering and in need.
Will I keep faith, that's the question?
Will I live each day in the belief that God is there,
sharing the pain,
the anguish,
the sorrow
and striving through it all to bring healing?

When life brings me down,
breaking the body and crushing the spirit,
will I still be able to lift up my head in confident hope,
assured that in the fullness of time –
God's time –
heaven will come on earth?

Silence

Prayer Living Lord,
whatever life brings,
however demanding it may prove,
and no matter how hard it may sometimes be
to understand your will
or to glimpse your hand at work,
help us to keep faith in your purpose,
to trust in your love
and to look forward to the dawn of your kingdom,
living each day in the light of that promise.
Amen.

Hymn Of the Father's love begotten

Closing prayer Gracious God,
just as you came to our world in Christ,
help us now to go out for you,
to proclaim his word,
share his love
and work for his kingdom.
Help us to live in him
and for him
and through him,
until that day when he comes again
and you are all in all.
Amen.

Christmas

Christmas (1)

Suggested visual material

Jesus of Nazareth 1
The Life of Christ I
Come, let us adore

Introduction

Few stories have been told as often as the one we celebrate today: that of the birth of Christ. The rest of the Bible may be all but ignored in our modern world, but not the people and events of this special season. They feature in nativity plays up and down the country: Mary, Joseph, shepherds, wise men, the innkeeper, and of course the baby Jesus at its heart. But are those anything more to us than names from long ago? For all too many the answer is no, and even when the answer is yes, the underlying reality may be different than we like to think. The very familiarity of the Christmas story can close our minds to its message, its immediacy and power to communicate being diluted through repetition. Today, then, we attempt to transport ourselves back across the centuries to that night when Jesus was born. We imagine what it must have been like to be there in the stable or out in the fields, to have seen in that newborn child the fulfilment of God's promises, and in his unfolding life to have heard God's voice. Ask yourself not just what it must have meant to those involved at the time, but what it means to *you* today.

Opening prayer

Gracious God,
at this time of giving,
help us to offer the worship, thanksgiving,
service and witness
that you alone deserve.
At this time of receiving,
help us to open our hearts to your gift of Christ,
making his love and life our own.
At this time of joy,
help us to celebrate the good news at its heart,
the wonder of your coming in Christ,

walking our earth and sharing our humanity.
At this time of sharing,
help us to reach out to those whose hearts are heavy,
crushed by hunger, poverty, sorrow and pain.
At this *special* time,
open our lives to your transforming power,
your love that is able to make all things new.
Take what we are,
and direct what we shall become.
Amen.

Hymn Good Christians all, rejoice

Comment The words of Matthew, which we will hear shortly, remind us of perhaps the most-forgotten person in the Christmas story: Joseph. He's there, of course, in our nativity plays, our Christmas cards, our readings and carols, but it's Mary, shepherds and wise men, and even the innkeeper who tend to steal the limelight, leaving poor old Joseph as some shadowy figure in the background. Yet *his* story, as much as anyone's, has lessons to teach us, not least about having the faith and humility to accept God's will, however uncomfortable that might be. Put yourself in his shoes and imagine the mixed emotions he must have wrestled with, the natural inclinations he must have felt. But reflect also on his final response. Are you as open as he was to what God wants to do in your life? Are you ready to follow his guidance rather than your own way?

Music *As Joseph was a-walking (Music for Advent and Christmas)* Margaret Rizza

Reading Matthew 1:18–25

Meditation of Joseph

I resolved to get rid of her
the moment she broke the news,
the thought of someone else's child growing within her
filling me with rage
and setting my head buzzing with plans
to put her aside.
It was a shock, be fair,

for I hadn't touched the girl,
let alone *slept* with her,
but if not me, then who?
The gossips would have a field day, that was for certain,
spreading first one story, then another,
and I didn't fancy that one bit.
So I made up my mind to hush things up,
break off the engagement quietly
and brush the whole sorry business under the carpet –
you can't get fairer than that.
As soon as I could, I'd tell her the score,
gently but firmly spell things out.
Only I never got the chance,
for God had other ideas,
not just for me but for everyone.
He was coming into our world,
my Mary chosen to bear the promised Messiah,
and, for all my doubting her,
all my unworthy thoughts,
I also had a part to play,
the privilege of helping to nurture his Son.
I'd made up my mind,
decided what I had to do,
but that night I learnt a vital lesson:
though *we* may make our plans,
it's *God* who directs our steps.

Silence

Prayer We can't help it, Lord.
Time after time,
day after day,
we look at life from *our* point of view
rather than from *yours*,
judging things by human standards,
from the perspective of this world.
Where *you* see possibilities,
we see problems.
When you speak,
we fail to hear.
While you try to lead us,
we resist and rebel.

Thank you that,
despite our struggle to glimpse your presence
and to recognise your hand at work,
you continue to work out your purpose,
patiently prompting and guiding,
and somehow in all things working together for good.
Teach us,
lead us,
take us,
use us,
by your grace
and for your glory.
Amen.

Hymn In the bleak mid-winter

Comment Responding to God's guidance – if that was true of Joseph it's equally so of the magi, and in more ways than you might imagine. We all know the story of how they saw the star in the East and followed it to Jerusalem, and then how – having first spoken with Herod – they travelled on to Bethlehem where they found the boy Jesus. Was their journey over? Not a bit of it. It had only just begun – a truth symbolised by a little detail Matthew includes at the end of their tale: 'they left for their own country by another road'. Why? Because God had warned them not to return to Herod. But I suspect it points to more than that, for what they saw in Bethlehem must have had a huge impact on them. They knelt there, remember, before a little child, presenting priceless and precious gifts, each of them clearly aware that they were privileged to share in a truly special moment, touched by the divine. Could they just have gone back home afterwards as though nothing had changed? Surely not. What they saw and experienced in Christ must have transformed the course of their lives for ever, just as it does for all who truly meet and know him.

Music *Zwar ist solche Herzensstube (Christmas Oratorio)*
J. S. Bach

Reading Matthew 2:1–12

Meditation of one of the magi

We left by another road,
a different route completely.
Oh I don't just mean our journey back East,
though yes, in that too we revised our travel plans.
It went much deeper:
our very lives changed direction,
somehow transformed the moment we saw that child.
He wasn't what we were expecting –
not at all –
nothing about his situation
speaking of grandeur and glory,
the trappings of a king,
yet we instinctively knelt before him in homage,
conscious that here was someone utterly unique,
special,
his birth of cosmic significance,
destined to shape not just the course of history
but eternity beyond.
Don't ask how we knew –
we just *did*, deep within,
each of us aware from the moment we saw that star
that we'd been touched by heaven,
privileged to witness the start of something greater
than we could comprehend.
So we followed,
and acclaimed the child,
offering our gifts in awestruck worship…
and we left as different people,
our lives turned round for ever
by a glimpse of the divine.
You think that fanciful?
Perhaps.
Yet believe me, if you were to meet him –
truly meet him for yourselves –
then the course of *your* life, too, would be changed.

Silence

Prayer Lord Jesus Christ,
we talk of the difference you make to our lives,
of how following you involves a change in direction,
taking *your* way rather than our own.
And we know it's true.
But though we start out with the best intentions,
we get deflected from our path
and go astray.
Help us, through your Spirit,
to meet you afresh each day,
experiencing firsthand the wonder of your grace,
goodness and love.
Open our hearts to a touch of the divine,
a glimpse of your glory,
so that the change you bring in us
may be real and lasting,
the course of our lives transformed now
and for all eternity.
Amen.

Hymn Infant holy

Comment How many Christmas presents this year will end up stuffed in the back of a drawer or cupboard, or donated to a charity shop? Almost certainly, more than a fair few. In this season of goodwill we feel almost duty bound to indulge in a frenetic spending spree, buying a little something for all kinds of people simply because it's the done thing, and buying masses more for family and friends in a bid to make this time special. It's all done with the best of intentions, but the result, sadly, is a mass of unwanted gifts. Many of our carefully chosen purchases are simply not needed. The opening verses of John's Gospel speak of another unwanted gift – that of God's love in Christ – but the irony is that this is something we all need, whoever we may be. In him is the secret to life, the answer to our inner emptiness, the one who makes possible new beginnings for all. Yet today – just as it has been across the centuries – many are not interested, turning their backs on what God would have them receive. What of you? Have you accepted what he offers? And do you continue to make it yours?

Music *In the Lord is my joy (Music for Advent and Christmas)* Margaret Rizza

Reading John 1:1–14

Meditation of John the Evangelist

It still puzzles me,
even as I write the words;
still leaves me mystified
that the world did not know him,
and that he was rejected, even by his own people.
But I've seen with my own eyes that it's all too true.
Not entirely, of course,
for some received him, Jew and Gentile alike –
a few ready to hear, listen and respond –
but they were the exception,
rarities;
for each individual who accepted his claims,
there were hundreds who turned their backs on him,
closed in heart and mind.
He offered them light
and they preferred darkness;
life, and they chose death.
Instead of being children of God,
born not of the flesh but of Spirit,
they dismissed the idea out of hand,
without, apparently, so much as a second thought.
There are many reasons why,
and it's not for me to judge –
he made that clear enough –
but it still leaves me amazed sometimes
that the one we longed to see over so many years
should be hounded to his death when he finally came.
Should I marvel, though?
Perhaps not,
for though his way brings unparalleled joy,
it brings cost too,
a price as well as reward.
It means give as well as take,
preferring *his* will to our own,

and, whoever we are,
that's more difficult than we might first imagine.
We've seen his glory,
that of God's only Son, full of grace and truth,
but never be complacent,
assuming that the job's done,
everything signed and sealed,
for we must go on responding day after day.
Some received him,
others would not;
some believed,
many didn't.
Ask yourself,
carefully,
prayerfully:
what about you?

Silence

Prayer Lord Jesus Christ,
help us to make room for you in our lives,
not at the margins,
allowed in when it suits us,
but at the heart of everything we think, say and do,
so that your guidance may direct our steps,
your purpose restore our hope
your mercy renew our faith,
and your love fashion our being.
Whatever else we allow to be squeezed out of life
teach us to welcome you afresh into our hearts,
today and every day.
Amen.

Hymn O little town of Bethlehem

Comment Can a story speak to us when we've heard it time and again? In a sense, no; it will never quite have the freshness it had on first hearing. But when it comes to the story of Christ – whether of his birth, his life, or his death and resurrection – we will find that if we look deeper there is always more to discover, new insights to be teased out, details that we'd previously overlooked suddenly leaping out at us from the page. Why? Because *this* story is not confined to the written word but concerns the Word made flesh, speaking not simply of what happened once, but of what's happening now; not just of what God has done but of what he continues to do. The one who was born in Bethlehem can be born also in you. What was good news for some is good news for all. As the Apostle John reminds us, the story of Jesus is special, for if we respond and receive, it is also *our* story.

Music *Break forth, O beauteous morning light (Christmas Oratorio)* Handel

Reading John 1:15–18

Meditation of the Apostle John

He made a difference to *me*, that's for sure,
his call transforming my life and making me new,
as though I've been born again.
How?
By showing me God,
making the divine real here on earth,
the Word made flesh.
Everything he did and said spoke of the Father,
bridging the gap between us
and making possible a living daily relationship,
not just for *me* but for *you* too,
for all the world!
There are no limits to his love,
no boundaries to his grace:
he wants to make a difference to everyone, everywhere,
pouring out his goodness to the ends of the earth.
'The true light,' he called himself,
shining in the darkness –
and that's certainly been so for me,
his love,
his goodness,
shining unfailingly into my life:
a lamp to my feet
and light to my path.
What about you –
have *you* seen the light too?

Silence

Prayer Lord Jesus Christ,
come amongst us now,
for so often we look around and see only darkness –
a shadow over our lives,
denying hope and destroying life.
Come into our hearts,
our homes,
our country,
our world,
and shine upon us,
so that we might bathe in the glow of your love
and the radiance of your grace,
your light scattering the darkness for ever.
Amen.

Hymn Hark, the herald-angels sing

Closing prayer Lord Jesus Christ,
help us to welcome, honour, love and serve you.
Teach us to know your truth,
do your will
and walk your way;
to acknowledge our faults,
receive your mercy,
and respond to your cleansing touch.
Equip us to work for you,
witness for you,
live for you,
today and every day.
Amen.

Christmas (2)

Suggested visual material

Jesus of Nazareth 1
The Life of Christ I
Come, let us adore

Introduction

A stable, a manger, a baby wrapped in strips of cloth – from Christmas carols to nativity plays such details are intimately associated with the birth of Jesus. Together with Mary and Joseph travelling to Bethlehem, shepherds hurrying from their fields by night and magi following a star, they are part of the magic of this season. But behind the romance of the story, what do they have to say to you and me today: about life now, the people we are and lives we lead? That's what we're going to explore today through a series of readings and reflections designed to take us back to that first Christmas over two thousand years ago. Imagine yourself in the shoes of some of those directly involved in the events of that night – Mary, shepherds, even one of the sheep! – and consider afresh the message of the nativity and its relevance for you, here and now.

Opening prayer

Gracious God,
we have heard, countless times,
the story of your coming,
perhaps so often that it fails to speak as it once did.
We hear the words,
sing the carols,
listen to the message,
without really taking it in,
familiarity blunting its force.
Help us to hear it again today
as though for the first time,
to take ourselves back in heart and mind to Bethlehem
and to the events surrounding the birth of your Son,
so that you may speak to us afresh,
just as you spoke then,
making known the immensity of your love

and your gracious purpose for all,
through Jesus Christ our Lord.
Amen.

Hymn Christians awake! Salute the happy morn

Comment The example of Mary at the annunciation is surely second to none as a source of inspiration to Christians across the years. Her humility, faith, courage and obedience are held up as a model to emulate, a paradigmatic response to the call of God. We can read the story time and again, yet still get more from it, for there are always fresh insights to be unearthed, new lessons to be learnt, unexplored angles to consider. Consider her response again now, so that it may more fully help to shape your own.

Music *A hymn to the Mother of God* John Taverner

Reading Luke 1:26–38

Meditation of Mary, mother of Jesus

Don't be afraid, he said!
As though angels popping up out of the blue
are two a penny,
no cause for concern.
Well I'm sorry, but I was petrified,
caught between the urge to run and scream.
And when he started on about being favoured by God,
blessed among women,
it only made things worse.
Who was *I* to be singled out,
I to be chosen –
a nobody like me from Nazareth?
Whoever this guy was, he'd come to the wrong house,
and the sooner he was gone the better.
But he *didn't* go,
and somehow, despite myself, I listened,
my amazement growing by the second
as he talked of a child I would bear;
a saviour who would rule over the house of David
and whose kingdom would never end.
'How can this be?' I asked.

'For a start, I'm still a virgin!'
But he wasn't finished yet, not by a long way,
this child he spoke of to be not just *my* son,
but *God's* too,
conceived by his Spirit.
Well, if I was troubled before,
I'd more reason to be then,
for this was mind-blowing stuff,
certain to turn the world upside down
and change my life for ever.
Yet somehow I suddenly felt strangely calm,
happy to accept whatever was asked of me,
no questions asked.
Why?
Because, if God was really speaking,
and could actually use someone as ordinary as me,
then surely *nothing* was beyond him,
however impossible it might seem.
The future was in *his* hands,
not *mine*,
and what better place could there be to leave it!

Silence

Prayer Mighty and mysterious God,
for all kinds of reasons we don't find faith easy.
We consider what is asked of us,
the scale of your challenge,
and we feel small,
incapable of rising to it.
We come up against questions of faith,
and we struggle for answers,
so much seeming to defy explanation.
And though part of us longs to serve you,
another part rebels,
preferring to serve self instead,
resisting your call and turning from your way.
Help us, despite everything that fights against you,
that deflects us from the path of faithful discipleship,
to stay true nonetheless.
Give us courage, confidence and conviction

to understand what you want from us
and gladly to respond.
Amen.

Hymn Born in the night, Mary's child

Comment The story of the shepherds hurrying to Bethlehem provides us with one of the iconic images of the nativity, recalled and re-enacted by generations since. We'll consider things from their perspective shortly, but first let us take a different and somewhat more unusual approach. Imagine if the sheep had somehow been able to reflect on their experience during that memorable night. Imagine if they could communicate what it felt like to be suddenly abandoned and left to fend for themselves, and the sense of relief they must have felt when the shepherds finally returned. It's a tantalising idea.

Music *L'enfance du Christ (The Shepherds' Farewell)* Berlioz

Reading Luke 2:1–15

Meditation of the sheep

1 I've never seen them move so fast –
one moment sprawled round the camp fire,
and the next up and off into the night –
heading for Bethlehem I think they said.

2 Well, sheep we may be,
but even *we* knew something was afoot,
something momentous,
truly special,
for they've never abandoned us before,
not even for a second,
what with wolves and the like prowling
in the darkness.

3 We were terrified –
more even than when that strange light
had appeared in the sky,
causing them to grovel in the dust,
then dash off like men possessed –
for we heard howling in the distance . . .
nearer . . .
nearer still . . .

until the shadows took shape . . .
ready to pounce . . .
anticipating their kill.

4 We waited for the end,
hot breath upon us,
slobbering jaws gaping wide,
but suddenly . . .
voices . . .
laughter . . .
and the danger gone –
the shepherds were back at last!

1 What relief!

2 What joy!

3 What delight!

4 We'd faced death and been saved!

2 But I tell you what,
something very strange:
those shepherds seemed happier still,
beside themselves with excitement,
almost as if *they'd* been saved too.

1 What was it, I wonder, they saw that night?

3 It must have been good.

Silence

Prayer Gracious God,
help us not just to *hear* the message of Christ's birth
but to make it our own,
meeting him afresh,
responding to his grace
and welcoming him into our lives.
May we recognise more fully
what he means for us and for all –
what you accomplished
through his life, death and resurrection,
and what you continue to accomplish
in countless human hearts.
Grant that the child of Bethlehem –
the crucified saviour and risen Lord –
may be born in us today,
and that we may walk with him to our journey's end.
Amen.

Hymn Once in royal David's city

Comment A baby lying in a manger wrapped in strips of cloth – it doesn't sound that exciting, does it? Hardly sufficient, were we shepherds, to prompt us to forsake our flock and rush off to Bethlehem. And if that's all there had been to it, then that's perfectly true. It was a happy sight, no doubt; a heart-warming and pleasing scene to move even the hardest of hearts, but hardly one to set the pulse racing, the heart skipping a beat. But that, of course, is to miss the point, for this was no run-of-the-mill birth, no ordinary child. He was the Messiah, God's promised deliverer, come at last to his people. The years of waiting were over, patience finally rewarded. The kingdom of God was at hand. No wonder the shepherds hurried off as fast as their legs could carry them, and raced back afterwards intent on telling everyone they met just what it was they'd seen. Our next reading and meditation explore their story.

Music *Infant holy (traditional carol)*

Reading Luke 2:15–20

Meditation of the shepherds

It was just as the angel had told us,
down to the very last detail:
the stable,
the manger,
even the strips of cloth,
and above all, of course, the child,
lying there so peaceful,
his exhausted mother looking on,
husband by her side.
I'll never forget that look in their eyes:
pride naturally, like every parent –
joy, relief, excitement –
but more than that,
an air of awe and reverence,
as if they couldn't quite take it in.
And as we talked with them,
sharing what we'd heard and seen,
we could understand why,

for *they'd* been told what *we* had –
that this boy of theirs was sent by God,
the promised Messiah,
saviour of the world!
We'd hardly dared credit it,
and neither it seems had they,
but the more we heard
and the more we listened,
the more indisputable it seemed.
We'd come, hoping,
longing to believe
yet not sure that we could.
We left, singing,
called to believe,
and quite certain that we *should*.

Silence

Prayer Saviour Christ,
thank you for promises of old foretelling your coming,
for the testimony of the Gospels
to your birth in Bethlehem,
for the witness of Scripture
to your life-changing power,
for the experience of those across the ages
called to be your Church.
But, above all,
thank you that we can know you for ourselves,
believing not just *about* you but *in* you
as we joyfully respond to your love.
You have called us to an adventure of faith.
Help us to embark on it with you.
Amen.

Hymn Silent night

Comment The accounts of the nativity, whether of Luke or Matthew, are written from the perspective of those directly involved – Mary, Joseph, shepherds, magi – and in their immediacy they capture the sense of joy and wonder that characterised the night of Christ's birth. John's Gospel approaches things from a different angle, the Evangelist – years after the event – beginning his account of the life of Christ by reflecting on the wider meaning of his coming. He does so from the context not only of his birth, but also of his death, resurrection and ascension, the child born in Bethlehem seen from the start as someone of cosmic significance. In our final reading and meditation, we consider the insights John sought to share.

Music *Love came down at Christmas (traditional carol)*

Reading John 1:1–18

Meditation of John the Evangelist

What's it all about, they ask me?
What does Jesus bring that we didn't have before?
Well, I've thought about that over the years,
pondered what it is that makes him so special,
and if I had to sum it up in one word,
it would be this:
grace!
That's what sets him apart from all others,
what makes the difference
between the old and the new.
Moses brought us the Law,
precious undoubtedly,
serving us well for centuries,
but it put the onus on us living up to it –
our observing its decrees and performing its rituals,
following its prescriptions as best we could.
The way of Christ is so very different,
for it speaks of a new covenant
written not on tablets of stone but in our hearts –
a relationship with God based on what he has done
rather than anything we might do.
Yes, we fall short of what he wants us to be.
Yes, we fail him time and again.
Yes, we are unworthy of his love
and undeserving of mercy.
But none of that matters,
for God has made the running,
accomplished what we could never achieve
on our own.

Don't settle for less.
Don't struggle against the odds
to put yourself right with him,
striving somehow to earn his blessing.
Reach out and accept what he longs to give.
From his fullness we have all received . . .
grace upon grace.

Silence

Prayer Loving God,
we know we fall short,
that we repeatedly fail you,
that we have no right to your love
or claim on your mercy,
and such knowledge hangs heavy upon us,
filling us with frustration and remorse.
Yet we know also that you are slow to anger
and swift to forgive,
your desire being to pardon rather than punish,
to redeem, renew and restore.
For your grace revealed in Christ
and the fresh start you daily make possible
through him,
receive our praise.
Amen.

Hymn It came upon the midnight clear

Closing prayer Lord Jesus Christ,
born in Bethlehem,
come afresh to our world today –
to our towns and cities,
our fractured communities,
our divided nations,
our bleeding planet.
Lord Jesus,
born in a stable,
come afresh to the poor and homeless,
the disenfranchised,
the weak and vulnerable,
the outcast, oppressed and exploited.

Lord Jesus,
born to suffer and die,
come afresh to those who are sick,
those in pain,
those facing death,
those who mourn loved ones.
Lord Jesus Christ,
born in ages past,
be born in *us* today.
Amen.

Christmas (3)

Suggested visual material

Jesus of Nazareth 1
The Life of Christ I
Come, let us adore

Introduction

A manger and stable, shepherds and magi – each are part of the traditional story of Christmas known and loved by us all. From school nativity play, to Christmas cards, to candlelight service, we encounter them again and again, yet still they have power to inspire and challenge, speaking of God with us, the Word made flesh, the birth of the Messiah, the fulfilment of God's promise and his gift of life. In this service, we attempt to put ourselves in the shoes of Mary, shepherds, magi and John the Evangelist, exploring what the events of Christ's birth meant to them and asking in turn what they mean for us.

Opening prayer

Almighty God,
like your servant Mary, we magnify your holy name,
praising you for the gift of Christ,
and committing ourselves to your service.
Like the shepherds, we come to meet him,
to celebrate the birth of our saviour
and respond for ourselves to his coming.
Like the magi, we bow in homage,
seeking to offer our worship,
our gifts,
our *selves*.
Like your people across the centuries,
we give thanks for this day,
rejoicing that the story we know and love so well
is able still to speak to our hearts;
that the one who was born among us
continues to bring new life to birth.
Draw among us through him,
and so draw us more closely to you.
Amen.

Hymn Love came down at Christmas

Comment Nothing sums up the spirit of Christmas better than the presents we give and receive. Why? Because, above all, this season is about the gift of God; his offer of new life in Christ and everything which that entails. He does not force this upon us but invites us to receive. He doesn't demand acceptance but encourages us to respond. And he goes on doing that day after day, asking if we will allow him to work in and through us to share his love and grace, and work towards the fulfilment of his kingdom. Have we, like Mary, fully understood the wonder of what that means?

Music *Ave Maria* Cuccini (arr. Prizeman)

Reading Luke 1:39–55

Meditation of Mary, mother of Jesus

They'll call me blessed,
most favoured among women,
and I can understand why,
for, incredibly, God has chosen *me* to bear his son,
me to carry the promised Messiah in my womb.
It's an honour beyond words,
a privilege no one could ever earn or deserve,
least of all me,
and I don't mind admitting
that I'm still reeling with the wonder of it all.
Yes, it will involve wagging tongues,
knowing winks,
disapproving glances –
and no doubt Joseph will have a thing or two
to say about it as well –
but however awkward or painful that may be,
it is more than worth it for the joy of being chosen
and of offering myself in the service of the Lord.
Yet don't think I'm the only one blessed –
that this awesome earth-changing birth
concerns simply me
and not others –
for if you imagine that, you couldn't be more wrong.
It's good news for all of us,

every man, woman and child:
news that will transform our lives,
our history,
the world itself.
For this child is sent by God to redeem his people:
to bring freedom, hope, joy and peace,
deliverance from whatever holds us captive,
and forgiveness for all our sins.
Think about what that means:
new life,
new beginnings –
an end to sorrow and suffering,
darkness and despair,
to death itself.
It's what we've longed to see and so long waited for,
the answer to our prayers.
So yes, they'll call me blessed,
but never forget that the blessing is equally yours –
God's gracious gift being for me,
for you,
for everyone.
My soul magnifies the Lord
and rejoices in God my saviour!

Silence

Prayer Lord Jesus Christ,
for your coming among us,
your gift of life,
and the peace, joy, hope and love you offer to all,
we worship you.
We praise you that you are still good news,
glad tidings not just for others
but for *us*.
With heart and soul,
all that we are,
together, we acclaim you.
Amen.

Hymn Child in the manger

Comment Which would you have remembered most had you been one of the shepherds: the light in the sky, the heavenly choir, the doting couple gazing into the manger, or the little child lying there among the straw? What would you have made of it all, and what would have lived with you afterwards – challenging, delighting and inspiring? As the following reading and meditation remind us, it's easy to forget just how overwhelming yet unforgettable their experience must have been.

Music *O holy night* Adolphe Adam

Reading Luke 2:1–20

Meditation of one of the shepherds

Surprised?
I should say so!
It's not every day, after all, that God comes calling,
announcing the birth of the Messiah –
and for us to be the first to hear of it,
the first to respond,
well, quite simply,
the very thought still takes my breath away.
But it wasn't only surprise we felt –
it was also fear, awe, amazement,
none of us quite knowing what to expect or do next.
You see, one moment there we were,
going about our usual business –
another uneventful night's work –
and the next, everything was different,
an incredible light filling the sky,
brighter than the brightest day,
seeming somehow to shine deep within,
searching, yet full of promise,
probing into the deepest corners of our minds,
yet at the same time
speaking of joy, peace, love and hope.
Yes, I know that sounds odd,
fanciful, you might say,
yet it's the best I can do,
that experience of ours
unlike anything we'd known before:

out of this world, but very much within it,
terrifying but thrilling,
mysterious but marvellous.
And after the light had faded,
and we'd hurried off to Bethlehem,
eager to see the truth of what we'd heard,
then the full wonder of it all became clear,
for in a ramshackle stable,
there among the hay,
watched over lovingly by his mum and dad,
was a child,
lying in a manger and wrapped in swaddling clothes,
just as the angel had said –
and about that place,
above all in his parent's eyes,
there was a light that spoke once again
of God's presence there,
as real and vibrant as out in those fields earlier.
We'd glimpsed God's glory,
not once but twice,
his presence among us breaking into our world –
breathtaking,
stunning,
overwhelming,
yet there by my side –
and I know now that this awesome God we serve
is greater than I'd begun to imagine
yet closer than I'd dared to dream,
his radiant love filling the heavens,
yet touching every part of life.

Silence

Prayer Thank you, Lord, for the wonder of your love,
always able to surprise us with joy
and with yet more reason to praise.
Thank you that you are higher
than our highest thoughts,
greater than we can ever comprehend,
the Lord and redeemer of all.

Help us,
this and every day,
to glimpse more of who and what you are,
to your praise and glory.
Amen.

Hymn While shepherds watched their flocks by night

Comment Strictly speaking, the magi belong to Epiphany rather than Christmas, their visit to Bethlehem taking place days, if not weeks, after the birth of Christ, yet in public consciousness they are wedded firmly to the Christmas story, so we too make room for them here. No doubt their experience of kneeling before Jesus must have been as memorable as that of the shepherds, yet they must also have been aware of a shadow hanging over things, embodied in the person of Herod and his enigmatic response to their search for the newborn king. What did he think? What did *they* think? And, equally important, what do *we* think?

Music *Three kings from Persian lands afar (Christmas carol)*
Peter Cornelius

Reading Matthew 2:1–12

Meditation of the magi

1 He seemed very interested, that king of theirs.
2 Almost *too* interested, we thought.
3 He'd every reason to be concerned, mind you.
2 After all, a newborn king represented a threat,
3 a rival,
1 a possible challenge to his rule.
3 Unless, of course, the child was his.
2 That's what we'd assumed –
1 well you would, wouldn't you? –
2 we'd fully expected to find the child
there in the palace.
1 But no, Herod hadn't the first idea
what we were talking about,
not when we first arrived,
3 just stood there, looking at us blankly,
trying to hide his bewilderment,

2 until his priests rooted around in their Scriptures
and turned up something about a child
being born in Bethlehem.
1 That's when Herod became all ears,
all attention,
urging us to hurry off and look carefully for the boy.
2 He wanted to pay him homage,
so he said,
but do you believe that?
1 *We* didn't.
3 Not having seen the expression in his eyes
as he sent us off.
1 Honestly, if looks could kill!
2 It was strange,
3 very strange . . .
2 for we'd come all that way expecting to find rejoicing,
1 celebrations,
3 a people gathering to welcome their king,
1 and instead we found them unprepared,
3 taken by surprise,
2 and if I'm not mistaken,
actually unwilling to receive him.
3 An event of cosmic significance
was taking place among them,
and they didn't want to know.
3 Amazing.
2 *You* wouldn't make that mistake, *would* you?
All *Would you?*

Silence

Prayer Lord Jesus Christ,
for our failure to welcome you as we should,
our keeping you at arm's length,
our resistance to your will,
forgive us.
Overcome our disobedience,
our apathy and weakness,
and help us to give you the place you deserve,
at the centre of our lives.
Amen.

Hymn We three kings of Orient are

Comment If Matthew and Luke give us the story of what the birth of Jesus meant to those most intimately involved as events unfolded, John takes another tack, spelling out what Christ's coming meant to him and means for all. The celebrated words with which he begins his Gospel speak of so much – grace, glory, truth, life, to name but some – but perhaps one theme dominates more than any other: that of light shining in our darkness. If anything sums up the essence of Christmas it is surely this.

Music *The Lord is my light (Fire of Love)* Margaret Rizza

Reading John 1:1–18

Meditation of John the Evangelist

'The light of the world', he called himself,
and after a lifetime following I can see why,
for he's lit up the lives of so many,
myself included,
offering a lamp for our path,
a lantern illuminating the way ahead.
Yes, there have also been darker moments,
times too many to number
when we've blundered about in confusion,
perplexed by the vagaries of this world
and struggling to reconcile our faith
with our daily experience.
And yes, on occasions we've felt lost,
uncertain where to turn next.
But somehow, just when the storm's at its fiercest,
the clouds break and we glimpse him again,
a ray of sunshine bursting through the gloom,
and we realise he was there all along –
prompting, providing,
supporting, guiding –
if only we'd had eyes to see.
I wish there were more moments like that –
moments when everything is clear and bright –
and one day I believe there will be,
a time coming when the light of his love

will flood our hearts
and bathe all in its radiance,
but until then we follow as best we can,
trusting that though the candle may flicker,
it will continue to burn –
a beacon of hope,
a flame of love,
the light of life!

Silence

Prayer Thank you, Lord, for being with us in *our* darkness,
your light continuing to shine
through trouble and tragedy,
turmoil and tears.
Break through where shadows still linger,
into our doubt and disbelief,
our disobedience,
our flawed commitment and weakness of will.
Illuminate all through the radiance of your love.
Amen.

Hymn O come, all ye faithful

Closing prayer Lord Jesus,
build your kingdom here on earth.
Saviour Christ,
rescue your people.
Light of the world,
scatter our darkness.
Prince of peace,
heal our wounds.
Lamb of God,
have mercy upon us.
Word made flesh,
make us new.
Emmanuel,
God with us,
come and be with us *all*.
Amen.

Epiphany

Epiphany (1)

Suggested visual material

Jesus of Nazareth 1
Jesus of Nazareth 2
The Life of Christ I
The Life of Christ II
Come, let us adore
Jesus, the Child

Introduction

Epiphany is not a word we often use, which perhaps is one of the reasons why this season tends to pass us by. So what does it mean? Think for a moment of waking up at the crack of dawn and watching the sun rise, gradually scattering the darkness and bathing the world in light and warmth. In other words, a fresh start full of promise, ushering in a new day. That's partly the idea behind the term. Think also of an expression we sometimes use – seeing the light – when the meaning of a puzzle we've been wrestling with for some time suddenly becomes clear, almost as though a curtain has been drawn back and the answer miraculously revealed. That too captures something of the sense of Epiphany. And this Christian season reminds us of how both such interpretations are fleshed out in the person of Jesus, in whom we see also the third meaning of epiphany: a manifestation of God. In Jesus, God with us, the Word made flesh, is the one who makes known the Father in a way no other can begin to. Today we celebrate all this, remembering how, in his own epiphany experience, Jesus stepped out of the shadows to start on the way that would lead from the Jordan to Jerusalem, from baptism to a cross; a journey into darkness that would bring light to the world.

Opening prayer

Gracious God,
illuminate our minds as we come to worship you.
Reveal to us afresh the wonder of your presence,
intensity of your love,
scope of your mercy
and extent of your purpose.

Open our hearts to know you better,
and to see your hand at work around us.
Speak now through this time of worship
and every day through the presence of your Spirit,
the fellowship of your people
and the riches of your word,
so that our lives may reflect the radiance of Christ,
the light of life.
Amen.

Hymn The race that long in darkness pined

Comment Epiphany is traditionally associated with the magi, and with good reason, for not only did they follow the light of a star to Bethlehem but in doing so they were seen by Matthew to have fulfilled the words of the prophet Isaiah (60:3): 'Nations shall come to your light, and kings to the brightness of your dawn.' Yet the immediate events after their departure paint a picture of unremitting gloom rather than of a radiant new dawn. Where is the joy, hope and blessing this child was meant to bring? Where are the new beginnings his coming promised? Here is a reminder, if any is needed, of the darkness into which the light shines, darkness that has not yet been fully overcome.

Music *Unto us a boy is born (fifteenth-century carol)*
from *Piae Cantiones*

Reading Matthew 2:13–23

Meditation of Mary, mother of Jesus

We had to pack our bags,
grab the baby
and run for it –
away from Bethlehem,
Judea,
the land we knew and loved,
and off to the arid deserts of Egypt.
That wasn't in the script, surely!
I'd expected joy at his birth,
mass celebrations,
even a fanfare of trumpets,

for wasn't our child Emmanuel,
God with us?
Why then were we slipping off into the night,
fleeing for our lives?
It didn't make sense.
Yet that's what we were told to do,
and good thing too,
for next thing we heard there was carnage back home,
a senseless slaughter of the innocents.
I'd imagined our son's birth meant an end to all that –
a new era of peace, harmony and justice –
yet the world appears as bruised and broken as ever.
Does God know what he's doing?
I hope so,
for his purpose seems to be hanging on a thread –
on one tiny child surrounded by darkness and danger.
You'd almost think he's ready to share not just our life
but also our death,
only, of course, that couldn't be . . .
Could it?

Silence

Prayer Lord Jesus Christ,
thank you for having reached out to all in need,
entering into our darkness in order to bring light.
Thank you for enduring hatred to show your love,
for facing death to bring life,
for bearing our sins to make possible forgiveness.
Come again into our broken world,
bringing healing to the sick,
justice to the oppressed,
guidance to the lost –
life to all.
Wherever hatred divides,
pain destroys
and evil defiles,
bring new beginnings
through your transforming touch,
and make us whole.
Amen.

Hymn The first Nowell

Comment Epiphany may begin with remembering the journey of the magi, but it starts in another and perhaps more meaningful sense with the baptism of Jesus in the Jordan. That was the moment he committed himself to the costly path ahead; the watershed that was to lead him along the way of sacrifice and service taking him from Nazareth to Jerusalem, from the wilderness to the cross. Why did he have to be baptised? Many have asked that question and put forward various answers. The meditation following our next reading explores one possibility.

Music *The Lord is my light and salvation (Music for Advent and Christmas)* Margaret Rizza

Reading Matthew 3:13–17

Meditation of John the Baptist

I was speechless at first,
my reaction a mix of horror and disbelief,
for how could I, John,
possibly baptise God's chosen one,
the Lamb sent to redeem the world?
It was preposterous,
and I very nearly refused,
desperate somehow to prevent him.
Surely *I* should have been asking *him*,
for I was unworthy even to loosen
the thong of his sandals,
to walk the same ground,
let alone do more.
But he insisted,
refusing to take no for an answer,
so eventually I relented and did what he asked.
I'm still puzzled though,
for I baptised as a sign of repentance,
of turning from sin,
and what had that to do with Jesus –
what faults had he to confess?
It was *we* who needed cleansing,
a fresh start,

changed lives –
us who time and again went astray.
Yet here he was, entering the water,
almost as if he could take *our* sin upon himself.
Could it be?
I know he came to bring forgiveness,
but to identify with us,
carry our load,
stand before God in our place –
surely not even *he* would do that!

Silence

Prayer Lord Jesus Christ,
we marvel at your love,
at the fact that you did not simply offer guidance,
instructions as to how we should live,
but instead identified yourself with us fully,
sharing our human vulnerability and weakness,
yet remaining without sin.
And though you withstood temptation to the very end,
you took upon yourself the punishment
that is rightfully ours,
cancelling out our sins on the cross.
Help us in response to that awesome commitment
to show at least a little of the same in return,
consecrating our lives to you in joyful service
and reverent praise.
Amen.

Hymn Jesus calls us o'er the tumult

Comment The commencement of his ministry meant a fresh chapter, not only for Jesus but also for those he called to follow him. Their meeting with Jesus marked the start of something that was to change their lives for ever; the first steps on a continuing journey of discovery, for this most amazing man revealed God to them in a way no other had begun to, bringing the divine down to earth.

For everyone who responds to the call of Christ, it's the same: a life-changing experience. Has that epiphany become real for you?

Music *Come, be with me (Sacred Dance)* Keith Duke

Reading John 1:29–42

Meditation of Andrew

'Come and see,' he said,
so we went to his lodgings
and remained there the rest of the day,
listening spellbound as he read the Scriptures
and brought them to life.
The Lamb of God, John had dubbed him,
and we soon realised why,
for he taught unlike any we'd heard before,
with quiet authority,
amazing insight
and awesome wisdom,
unfolding the Law and prophets
so that they spoke not just of the past but of the present.
Clearly God was with him –
but no, it was more than that:
he was speaking *to* and *through* him,
heaven somehow touching earth in his person,
the divine there beside us.
Could it be, we wondered?
Could he be the long-awaited Messiah,
the one we'd all so longed to see?
Surely so!
And we rushed off finally to spread the news,
to tell others of the one we'd found.
He told us to come,
to see for ourselves,
and, thank heaven, that's what we did.
We followed him home,
and we're following still,
for he's shown us the way to life.

Silence

Prayer Lord Jesus Christ,
help us to know you for ourselves,
to make time each day
to nurture a meaningful relationship,
dependent not on what others have told us –
on what we've learnt second-hand –
but on a personal encounter,
an ongoing experience of your presence.
Draw near,
and keep us close to you,
now and always.
Amen.

Hymn I want to walk with Jesus Christ

Comment We've touched already on the call of Peter, James and John, but in our next reading we will hear of it in more detail. What did that call actually involve? It wasn't just to renounce their old way of life, laying down their nets to follow him, though of course that was part of it. It was a summons to fish for people; in other words, to share their new life and faith, to pass on what they had received. And once again that goes on being true today for all who would follow him. We too are called to witness; not forcing our faith on others, but testifying as best we can through word and deed to what we have found in Christ. His light is not to be hidden under a lampshade but set up on a hill where it can shine into the world. Only then can others experience the epiphany of Christ for themselves.

Music *Here am I, Lord (Sacred Weave)* Keith Duke

Reading Matthew 4:12–23

Meditation of the Apostle James We were mending our nets:
dull work, perhaps, but a necessary evil,
for if they were broken we'd catch nothing
though we fished all day.
Each haul put food on the table
and clothes on our backs,
yet when Jesus called we didn't just break off

but left them behind,
discarding our livelihood
with barely a backward glance.
Madness, some called it,
but it was the best move we ever made,
for it wasn't just our nets that were broken
but our lives,
our world,
and he alone could put things right.
I knew it somehow the moment I met him,
his very presence tugging at my heart
and touching my soul.
We were overwhelmed, all of us,
feeling unworthy to respond yet unable to resist,
and as we walked and talked with him in days to come
so that sense grew stronger,
for he revealed our needs . . .
yet also answered them,
exposed our faults . . .
yet brought forgiveness and new beginnings,
inner healing as undeniable as it was undeserved.
We've no nets now,
but we're fishing nonetheless,
this time for people,
for we want others to experience what we've found,
to taste his joy and share his life –
to know that, however broken they may be,
his love can make them whole.

Silence

Prayer Lord Jesus Christ,
we don't understand everything about you –
our knowledge being partial and limited.
We haven't fully grasped the meaning of discipleship,
what it will ask of us,
what it will cost.
We struggle to walk your way,
so easily being led astray by temptation.
We fail to give you the place in our lives you deserve,
allowing you to be crowded out by more immediate
but ultimately irrelevant concerns.

Our faith is weak
and our commitment poor,
yet we know that in you alone
lies the answer to our needs:
the way,
the truth
and the life.
Help us to hear your call
and to follow.
Amen.

Hymn Lord, the light of your love is shining

Closing prayer Saviour Christ,
shine in the darkness of our world –
into our sorrow, hurt, pain and despair.
Scatter the clouds that hang over us –
the shadows of hatred, violence and war.
Break into the night-time of evil and injustice,
and bring among us a new dawn.
Illumine the way of all who cry out
for a lamp to their feet
and light to their path.
Bathe us in the sunshine of your love.
Amen.

Epiphany (2)

Suggested visual material

Jesus of Nazareth 1
Jesus of Nazareth 2
The Life of Christ I
The Life of Christ II
Come, let us adore
Jesus, the Child

Introduction

If Advent is the poor relation compared to Christmas, then Epiphany is the forgotten cousin, most people having little idea as to what this season signifies. It's seen, if anything, as a winding-down from Christmas, a last chance to sing the odd carol as we remember the story of the magi before looking ahead to the rest of the Christian year. And that's not entirely wide of the mark, for this is indeed a time that invites us to reflect further on the Christmas message and what it means. But it's much more than that, for above all it speaks of the unfolding revelation of God in Christ to those with ears to hear and eyes to see: those like John the Baptist; Peter, James and John and the rest of the apostles; and those who flocked in such numbers to hear Jesus' message, receive his touch and witness his power. It was clear to these that he was someone different, special; someone who not only *talked* about God but revealed his true nature, his loving purpose for all. That's what Epiphany is about: recognising afresh the glory of God in Christ. And that's what this service invites us to do: through prayer, song, readings and reflection, to encounter again the Word made flesh, the one in whom the divine has become human and light from heaven been brought down to earth.

Opening prayer

Almighty God,
thank you for making yourself known to us in Christ.
You are above and beyond us,
defying definition,
and yet you took flesh and entered our world,
revealing yourself in human form.

Help us to glimpse your glory –
to discern your power,
experience your love,
receive your mercy
and know your peace.
Illuminate our lives with the light of your love,
shining *on* us,
in us
and *through* us,
by the grace of your Son,
Jesus Christ our Lord.
Amen.

Hymn Light of the world! forever, ever shining

Comment The journey of the magi – it's one of the most familiar and best loved stories of the Bible; one that has captured the imagination of countless generations. Who were these men? Where did they come from? How far did they travel? We can't definitively answer such questions, but one issue we can at least explore is why they followed the star and what they hoped to find at their journey's end. Were they eager merely to gawp at a newborn king, or was their something deeper going on beneath the surface? We're going to explore one possible answer.

Music *We three kings (traditional carol)*

Reading Matthew 2:1–12

Meditation of the magi

1 We weren't just looking for a child –
we were searching for *meaning,*
an answer to the riddle of life.
2 That's why we'd spent so long studying the stars,
poring over ancient texts,
seeking knowledge,
for we wanted to understand why we're here,
and whether there's anything
beyond our brief existence,
giving purpose to it all.

3 So we left our country,
and travelled,
mile after mile,
following that star –
not sure where it would lead,
not clear it would lead *anywhere*,
but hoping, believing, it was a sign,
portending a newborn king.

1 We were right too,
though it wasn't ultimately the star leading us;
it was God –
God as we'd never known him before:
mighty and mysterious,
sovereign over all,
yet somehow there in a little child
before whom we instinctively bowed in worship.

2 I can't explain it,
for he was just a kid,
yet each of us, as we knelt before him,
knew he was much more –
the goal not just of our journey
but of our lifelong quest,
our restless longing for truth.

3 Strangely, others didn't see it that way,
even his own people,
though whether they *couldn't* or *wouldn't*,
who can say?
All I know is this:
that we had questions
and found answers,
learning that those who seek
will find.

Silence

Prayer Living God,
in a world where so many search for meaning,
where people feel lost and hopeless,
confused about who they are,
why they are here
or what they should do,
give guidance.

Prompt and challenge through your Holy Spirit,
so that those who long for answers may find in Christ
an end to their seeking –
their questions resolved and lives fulfilled.
Amen.

Hymn We three kings of Orient are

Comment Why was it that John the Baptist was happy to play a supporting role, to point away from himself and towards Jesus? His ministry, after all, was causing a sensation, crowds flocking to hear him from across Judea, so why not bask in the adulation? True, some feared rather than loved him, but all respected him as a prophet sent by God. Yet that's the key to understanding how John saw himself, for he was indeed a prophet – called, in other words, to declare the message entrusted to him by God. He could speak of God's kingdom, announce its coming, but he could not bring it about. He could proclaim the need for repentance and changed lives, but he was unable to help people to be actually different. The fresh start they needed, the forgiveness and new beginnings, could be brought by one only: the saviour whose way he was called to make ready.

Music *O Thou that tellest (Messiah)* Handel

Reading Mark 1:4–11

Meditation of a follower of John the Baptist

They came in their droves,
hundreds arriving each day
eager to confess their faults and make amends.
There was no pretence,
no hiding their mistakes –
they knew they'd done wrong
and longed to start again.
So I did what I could,
baptising them as God had commanded
for the forgiveness of sins.
And were they pardoned?
Of course,

for ours is a God who delights to show mercy,
whose nature is always to forgive.
But a new beginning?
Nothing *I* could do could give them that,
nor anything *they* might do either,
for it takes something more –
a new heart and a right spirit,
change deep within.
Just imagine what that means:
no more striving on our own,
struggling to do what can't be done;
no more trying to earn what we can never deserve;
but God taking the initiative,
accepting what we are
and directing what we shall become.
It's been our hope,
our goal,
our dream for so many years,
foretold by the prophets yet always out of reach.
But not any more,
for Christ has come,
the redeemer of the world
who makes all things new.
I wash with water,
he with the Holy Spirit.
I cleanse the body,
he the soul.
We can really change,
truly start again.
Don't settle for less.

Silence

Prayer Lord,
we yearn to change,
try to do so,
but for all our best intentions we can't do it alone.
Our spirit says one thing,
our flesh another,
time and again weakness causing us to fall.
Forgive our faithless,
and, in your mercy,

write your law of love on our hearts,
so that we may know your will and delight to do it.
Amen.

Hymn O love, how deep, how broad, how high

Comment To whom or what does your life point? Do people see in you simply another person following the way of the world, or does something about you speak in some way of God? It's not just John the Baptist who was called to prepare the way of the Lord, helping others to recognise and receive him into their lives. As we'll see again now, that responsibility rests with us all.

Music *How beautiful are the feet (Messiah)* Handel

Reading John 1:1–14

Meditation of John the Baptist

They mistook me for the real thing, some people . . .
can you believe that?
A few of them –
no, more than a few –
actually thought I was the one they'd been waiting for:
the promised Messiah,
sent by God to redeem his people.
Well, I soon put them right on that,
for it was the last thing I wanted people to think,
the opposite of everything I'd been trying to say.
I was a servant, that's all,
my task being simply to prepare the way,
to make the path of the Lord that little bit easier
when he finally came,
and I was more than happy with that role,
counting myself privileged,
truly honoured,
to play some part in bringing his kingdom closer.
Did I succeed?
That's not for me to say,
but I did my best,
striving to point, in word and deed, away from myself
and towards him,
and if I helped even one person respond,

then it was worth it,
my job well done.
It's down to *you* now,
the torch yours to carry in turn,
for my journey, in this life at least, is nearly done.
He needs *you* now to speak for him,
your life to express his love and mercy,
and though you can't do that alone,
by his Spirit and in his strength
your witness *can* help others see him for themselves.
There's a limit, of course,
for his light shines brighter than we can even begin to,
but if you can reflect just a chink,
the merest glimmer of his radiance,
then, believe me,
you'll make a difference to someone, somewhere,
greater than you dare imagine.

Silence

Prayer Loving God,
help us in who and what we are,
in everything we think, do and say,
to point to you.
Move and work within us, so that,
despite everything that obscures your goodness,
we may make known your love,
share your compassion,
witness to your grace
and bring something of your light to those around us.
Teach us to know you better
and to become more like you,
through Jesus Christ our Lord.
Amen.

Hymn Thou whose almighty word

Comment Our next reading records the changing by Jesus of water into wine – an astonishing incident indeed. But for the writer of John's Gospel it was far more than that: not just a miracle but a sign. This was no crude attempt by Jesus to win hearts and minds, to wow people into following him. It was a pointer to who he was and what he'd come to do, a graphic demonstration of the way God's loving purpose was finding fulfilment through him. Here, as with so much in Scripture, if we look deeper we'll find more.

Music *Gloria in excelsis Deo (Gloria)* Vivaldi

Reading John 2:1–11

Meditation of a servant at the wedding feast in Cana

We put water into those jars, no doubt about it.
I should know, for I helped fill them up,
and I'm telling you straight,
there was nothing in them when we started
and nothing else added as we went along –
just pure, simple water.
Yet, when we drew off a cupful
and took it to the steward,
you should have seen his face.
A connoisseur he was,
and I've never seen anyone smack their lips
with such delight!
Next thing we knew
he'd dashed across to the bridegroom
and was slapping him on the back like an old friend,
all smiles and congratulations
for having saved the best till last.
Well, we thought at first he was having us on,
but when we tasted it ourselves
we realised what all the fuss was about,
for it was exquisite,
the sort of wine you'd serve at the finest banquet,
and we had gallons of the stuff to spare!
How did it happen?
I haven't the foggiest!
We just followed instructions,
and Jesus did the rest,
turning the ordinary into the special,
the old into something wonderfully new.
You'll think that a miracle, no doubt,
and I couldn't agree more,
but it's nothing compared to what followed,

for since then he's changed not just *water* into wine,
but human lives,
the world itself,
transforming life and death by his touch.
I'll never forget that wedding feast –
the surprise,
the joy,
the wonder of it all –
but, more important,
I won't forget the one who made it possible:
that amazing man, Jesus.
'Do whatever he tells you,' his mum had said,
and it's the best advice I've ever had.
Follow that and, believe me,
you won't go far wrong.

Silence

Prayer Lord Jesus Christ,
thank you for your ability to change lives,
to transform even the most unlikely of people,
turning them upside down and inside out.
Thank you for having changed *our* lives,
filling them with hope, joy, peace and purpose.
Continue to bring new beginnings to all,
reaching out into our world
and, wherever there is pain, sorrow, evil and injustice,
accomplishing real and lasting change.
Amen.

Hymn Come and see the shining hope

Closing prayer Lord Jesus Christ,
as magi came to your light,
walking in faith to their journey's end,
help us to follow in turn,
your grace and truth offering a lamp to our path.
As John the Baptist greeted you as the Lamb of God,
sent to take away the sins of the world,
may we too welcome you,
joyfully receiving the forgiveness you so freely offer.
As the disciples responded to your call,

leaving their nets and fishing instead for people,
so may we consecrate ourselves to your service,
seeking in word and deed to walk your way
and testify to your saving grace.
As the multitude thronged around you,
eager to listen to your word
and witness your mighty deeds,
may we also hunger to hear your voice
and comprehend your glory –
to experience firsthand the wonder of your love.
Shine in our hearts, Lord,
and help us to know you better.
Amen.

Epiphany (3)

Suggested visual material

Jesus of Nazareth 1
Jesus of Nazareth 2
The Life of Christ I
The Life of Christ II
Come, let us adore
Jesus, the Child

Introduction

Christians forgetting Advent? Unlikely. Ignoring Christmas? Impossible! Celebrating Epiphany? *Unusual*. Or at least it is for some, this third season of the Christian year passing them by unnoticed – and that's a shame, for it speaks equally as powerfully as Advent and Christmas of the hope, joy, peace and blessing God offers in Christ. It takes us forward, having celebrated his birth, to the start of Jesus' ministry: his response to God's call; his mission not just to *bring* light, but to *be* light; his proclamation of God's kingdom; his transforming love, bringing new life from old. Reflect on those, ask what they mean, and this season can truly be an epiphany experience for you.

Opening prayer

Sovereign God,
we are here in the name of Christ.
Meet with us
and speak to us now,
through him.
Reveal to us more of his way:
what it means to know, love and serve him,
what he shows us of you,
what he has done for us all
and what he continues to do in our world.
Remind us of the new beginnings he makes possible,
his transforming love that takes what is
and determines what shall be.
Teach us of his kingdom in which the last will be first
and the least greatest,
your will done here on earth as it is in heaven.
Speak of how your word,

your promises
and your Law
find fulfilment in him;
and of his taking upon himself the punishment
that was rightfully ours,
sharing both our life and our death.
Sovereign God,
open our hearts,
and help us to glimpse more of your light, love,
grace and truth
made known in him.
Amen.

Hymn What child is this

Comment From the beginning, Jesus was met with different responses: acceptance by some, rejection by others – a curious mixture of love and hatred, welcome and opposition, that greeted him throughout his ministry. In few places does that contrast stand out more clearly than in the encounter described in our next reading: on the one hand, magi, so determined to worship the newborn Christ that they'd journeyed for miles to find him; and on the other, Herod, his attitude altogether different.

Music *Three kings from Persian lands afar (Christmas carol)*
Peter Cornelius

Reading Matthew 2:1–12

Meditation of the magi

1 He seemed very interested, that king of theirs.
2 Almost *too* interested, we thought.
3 He'd every reason to be concerned, mind you.
2 After all, a newborn king represented a threat,
3 a rival,
1 a possible challenge to his rule.
3 Unless, of course, the child was his.
2 That's what we'd assumed –
1 well you would, wouldn't you? –
2 we'd fully expected to find the child
there in the palace.

1 But no, Herod hadn't the first idea
what we were talking about,
not when we first arrived,
3 just stood there, looking at us blankly,
trying to hide his bewilderment,
2 until his priests rooted around in their Scriptures
and turned up something about a child
being born in Bethlehem.
1 That's when Herod became all ears,
all attention,
urging us to hurry off and look carefully for the boy.
2 He wanted to pay him homage,
so he said,
but do you believe that?
1 *We* didn't.
3 Not having seen the expression in his eyes
as he sent us off.
1 Honestly, if looks could kill!
2 It was strange,
3 very strange . . .
2 for we'd come all that way expecting to find rejoicing,
1 celebrations,
3 a people gathering to welcome their king,
1 and instead we found them unprepared,
3 taken by surprise,
2 and, if I'm not mistaken,
actually unwilling to receive him.
3 An event of cosmic significance
was taking place among them,
and they didn't want to know.
3 Amazing.
2 *You* wouldn't make that mistake, *would* you?
All *Would you?*

Silence

Prayer Lord Jesus Christ,
for our failure to welcome you as we should,
our keeping you at arm's length,
our resistance to your will,
forgive us.
Overcome our disobedience,

our apathy and weakness,
and help us to give you the place you deserve,
at the centre of our lives.
Amen.

Hymn As with gladness men of old

Comment Why did Jesus need to be baptised? That's the question that rose immediately to the lips of John the Baptist the moment he saw Jesus approaching him. The baptism John practised symbolised repentance; a turning from the old self to the new, but surely neither of those applied to Jesus. He had nothing to be cleansed of, no need to start again. Yet Jesus believed baptism was necessary nonetheless, so let us consider for a moment what, for him, was clearly a pivotal moment in his life.

Music *Total immersion (Sacred Pathway)* Keith Duke

Reading Luke 3:15–17, 21–22

Meditation of John the Baptist

Did I imagine it:
the voice from heaven,
dove descending from on high?
I might have done,
for it was an emotional moment,
not just for me
but for him too.
He'd come to me there by the Jordan,
and I knew at once who he was,
something about him speaking unequivocally of God.
He was the Messiah,
the one whose way I'd been sent to prepare,
and I was overwhelmed with the honour, wonder and joy of it all.
He, of course, should have baptised *me*,
for compared to him I was nothing,
but, for all my protestations, he insisted otherwise,
resolved to mark the start of his ministry through the waters of baptism.
Was it to honour the Law, perhaps?
To identify with humankind?

Or simply to symbolise a new chapter in his life?
I'm not sure.
But what I do know is this:
that he committed himself that day to the path ahead:
to the way of sacrifice, surrender and self-denial
that would bring life to the world.
He was ready to serve,
to fulfil his calling, whatever it took.
And whatever I may have imagined that day,
one thing's for sure:
God's hand was upon him,
delighting in the courage and commitment of this,
his beloved Son.

Silence

Prayer Lord Jesus Christ,
thank you that,
having committed yourself to the way of the cross,
you walked it faithfully,
to the very end.
Thank you for your courage and devotion,
your willingness to give you all.
Help us, in turn, to consecrate ourselves to you
and faithfully to follow,
honouring your call to discipleship
through an ongoing journey of faith.
Amen.

Hymn Brightest and best of the sons of the morning

Comment A revealing of the divine, manifestation of reality – that's how the dictionary defines the word 'epiphany', and that is precisely what we see in the turning of water into wine: the first sign, according to John the Evangelist, performed by Jesus to indicate who and what he was. It speaks of new from old, the fulfilment of the Law and prophets in the person of Christ. It speaks more deeply of the one who would offer himself for us, and for all.

Music *He turned the water into wine (The Gospel Road)*
Johnny Cash

Reading John 2:1–11

Meditation of Mary, mother of Jesus

It seemed a strange thing to say:
'My hour has not yet come.'
After all, I'd only casually mentioned
that they had no more wine.
So what did he mean, I wonder,
by that peculiar response of his?
Not that I let it worry me.
I knew my boy well enough to be sure he'd offer help,
for he never could see someone in need
and pass them by.
Sure enough, he came to the rescue,
producing not just fresh supplies for the party
but the best yet,
special enough for the most discerning palate.
I *should* have worried, though,
and *would* have done had I understood better,
for this was just a foretaste of things to come,
that hour Jesus spoke of calling, in time,
for new wine of a different sort:
his blood shed for many,
poured out for the forgiveness of sins,
spilled on the cross as he suffered and died for all.
Truly, indeed, the best was saved till last,
the water of the Law and prophets transformed
into the fruit of the true vine,
but at what cost,
what sacrifice,
what sorrow!
Back there, in Cana, that was all in the future,
unknown to all but him,
so we ate, drank and made merry.
He alone knew what was coming,
the awful price he'd be asked to pay
that we might feast with him in heaven.
He saw our need,
he knew what he must do,
and, once again, he couldn't say no.

Silence

Prayer
Forgive us, Lord,
for too often we say no to others
and no to you.
We see situations of need around us,
but we hold back,
whether through apathy,
selfishness
or fear of getting involved.
Remind us of what you endured,
what you sacrificed,
to transform our broken world,
and give us faith, love and commitment
to, in some small way, respond in turn.
Amen.

Hymn Hills of the north, rejoice

Comment According to an old saying, 'There's none so blind as those who will not see.' Truth may be staring us in the face, but if we close our eyes to it then it will pass us by. And, of course, that can go for the truth revealed in Jesus as much as any other; in fact, perhaps there most of all, for rather than face the challenge he brings many prefer to evade it. As we reflect now on words from the Gospel of Luke, let us ask ourselves whether we are as open as we like to imagine to what God would show us.

Music *All you nations (Awakening in Love)* Margaret Rizza

Reading Luke 4:14–21

Meditation of a member of the synagogue in Nazareth
We knew what he was going to say,
even before he said it,
and if at first we'd been filled with pride,
delighted to hear one of our own read so beautifully,
in a trice it all changed,
our mood changing to anger
at the sheer presumption of the man.
There had been a note of challenge in his voice
from the start,

as though he understood those words of Isaiah
as applying directly to himself
and was daring us to suggest otherwise.
So when he returned the scroll and sat back down,
our eyes never left his,
nor his ours.
It was like a battle of wills,
a test of strength:
who would dare to lay things on the line first?
Eventually, it was Jesus who broke the silence,
confirming our worst suspicions.
'Today,' he said,
'this scripture has been fulfilled in your hearing',
implying it was somehow realised in him!
What rubbish!
We knew who this man was,
having seen him grow up among us,
suckle at his mother's breast,
labour in his father's workshop –
he was just an ordinary person like you and me.
So what gave him the right
to put on such airs and graces?
Okay, so he'd caused a stir in the surrounding villages
with a few signs and wonders,
and maybe he did know the Scriptures better than the rest of us,
but that didn't make him God's gift, did it!
He came up eventually with some fancy line,
suggesting that a prophet is without honour
in his own country,
as though this somehow proved his point.
But it didn't, not to my mind,
for he was making himself out to be much more than a prophet:
the fulfilment, rather, of God's promises of old.
No, we'd have recognised a prophet all right,
but for him to be who he said he was,
sent and anointed by God,
he'd have had to be someone far greater –
the promised Messiah,
Son of God –
and, in all honesty, could anyone miss that?!

Silence

Prayer Open our eyes, Lord, to the good in those around us,
those we know so well
that we can sometimes take them for granted.
Help us to recognise their gifts,
their qualities,
their contribution to our lives,
and to encourage them through genuine appreciation
of all that they do and are.
Amen.

Hymn God of mercy, God of grace

Comment As we'll hear in our next reading, almost as soon as Jesus was born, Mary and Joseph busied themselves with fulfilling the demands of the Law, taking him to be purified at the Temple as was the custom of the time. Did they know then that Jesus would one day die to fulfil the requirements of the Law in a very different sense? Probably not, despite what Simeon was to say to Mary concerning a sword piercing her soul. For her, as for us, the full wonder of what he came to do is revealed fully only in the light of the cross.

Music *And he shall purify (Messiah)* Handel

Reading Luke 2:22–40

Meditation of Mary, mother of Jesus

We did it all by the book,
presenting a sacrifice to the Lord.
It was what the Law demanded –
the blood of an unblemished offering
as a purification for sin –
and when all was properly done, we went home,
still marvelling at his gift of our son.
He *was* a gift too –
we'd known that from the start –
but what we hadn't fully grasped
is how much that gift would cost,
not *us* . . .
but *him*.

For, you see, he too was to honour the Law,
presenting a sacrifice to God,
only the offering was to be his own body,
broken for all.
We'd no inkling then, of course,
despite what that fellow Simeon had said in the Temple
about a sword piercing my heart.
We assumed, from what God had told us,
that Jesus would enjoy glory,
and so, in a sense, he would,
though not as the world understands such things –
his kingdom not being of this world,
his life shared through death.
He came not to deny the Law but to fulfil it,
my poor boy the pure unblemished lamb
making atonement for our sins.
No more need for doves and pigeons,
blood spilt on the altar,
for he would spill *his* instead,
surrendering everything to put us right with God.
Through him we are cleansed,
forgiven –
redeemed, renewed, restored.
He finished everything required by the Law,
and then returned from whence he'd come –
not to Galilee or Nazareth,
but to the Father's side.
And if I marvelled once at the gift of *our* son,
believe me, I marvel yet more at the gift of *his*!

Silence

Prayer Lord Jesus Christ,
we worship you,
we honour, acclaim and extol your name,
for you have done what we could never do alone:
reconciled us with God.
You offered yourself,
a perfect sacrifice,
taking our sins upon you
and nailing them to the cross –
debt cancelled,

price paid.
The barrier is broken,
hostility at an end!
Receive our grateful praise.
Amen.

Hymn The people that in darkness sat

Closing prayer Light of life,
shine upon us.
Light of truth,
shine within us.
Light of love,
shine from us.
Light of the world,
shine through us.
Lord Jesus Christ,
wherever there is darkness
shine your light,
and may it never be extinguished.
Amen.

Lent

Lent (1)

Suggested visual material

Jesus of Nazareth 2
Jesus of Nazareth 3
Jesus of Nazareth 4
The Life of Christ II

Introduction

Of all the seasons of the Christian year, probably none is as misrepresented and misunderstood as Lent – a time that is typically associated solely with sacrifice and self-denial – in other words, a stern and forbidding injunction to go without. That, of course, can have a valid place in Lenten observance, but it is by no means the sum total or even the focus of what Lent actually means, for, at its heart, this season is simply about consecrating time to God, setting aside a few weeks and seeking to make them special in terms of our relationship with him. We do so, not as an end in itself, but with a view to committing *all* of life to God, such that each moment of every day is touched by his presence. Through reflecting on how Jesus consecrated his life to the Father, both through his forty days and nights in the wilderness, and through his life and death beyond, let us seek his help to commit ourselves in turn to loving and joyful discipleship.

Opening prayer

Almighty God,
examine us,
and make up for where we are lacking;
test us,
and show where our commitment is weak;
speak to us,
and deepen our faith;
guide us,
and inspire us to follow;
challenge us,
and teach us to listen;
call us,
and help us to respond.
Take this season

and through it lead us closer to you,
so that we may become more nearly
the people you would have us be.
Amen.

Hymn O Lord we want to praise you

Comment For a few, responding to the call of Christ means renouncing the world and turning their backs on its pleasures. But is that asked of us all? Surely not. The monastic or contemplative lifestyle may be right for some, but if everyone pursued it, this world would soon find itself in trouble, society unable to continue in any recognisable shape or form. For all its faults and ugliness, we believe this world is God's gift, so much within it capable of moving us to joy, awe and thanksgiving. As our next reading and meditation remind us, Jesus never attempted to deny this, his concern rather being to warn us against losing our sense of perspective; from being so focused on earth that we lose sight of heaven.

Music *Christ before me (Music for Lent, Holy Week and Easter)* Keith Duke

Reading Matthew 6:1–6, 16–21

Meditation of a listener to Jesus

Treasures on earth?
Huh, no chance of that!
It's all I can do to make ends meet,
so if Jesus thinks I'm likely to be snared
by worldly wealth,
he's barking up the wrong tree.
Or is he?
For what, actually, do I most value,
enough to treasure it beyond all else?
If that's what he's asking,
suddenly my answer is very different,
for, pressed to choose between heaven and earth,
I'm afraid the second too often wins.
I may talk of costly commitment, and so forth,
but my time, money and energy goes into serving self,

or, at least, my loved ones,
rather than God.
This world *matters* to me,
so much within in it special beyond words,
and he believes that too, I'm sure of it.
Only he calls us to look deeper:
not simply to what enriches life,
but to what it's finally all about.
Put our hope in this world alone, he tells us,
confusing the gift with the giver,
creation with creator,
and our heart will inevitably be broken.
There are treasures on earth,
blessings to be received with thanks
and joyfully celebrated,
but none of them, however precious,
can satisfy our deepest need.
Only God can do that,
now and for eternity.

Silence

Prayer Creator God,
help us to celebrate this world you have given us,
but not too much;
to enjoy the blessings of life,
but not to pin our happiness upon them;
to make use of the abundant resources
you have put at our disposal,
but not to abuse them.
Help us to remember that gratifying the body
is not the same as satisfying the soul;
that riches on earth are very different
from treasures in heaven.
Teach us, then, to rejoice in all we have received now,
but to use it wisely,
lovingly
and responsibly,
setting our hearts above all
on the things of your kingdom,
through Jesus Christ our Lord.
Amen.

Hymn All my hope on God is founded

Comment The story of Jesus' time in the wilderness encapsulates what for many Lent is all about: temptation. But what does that mean for us today? Too often it's understood as a stick with which we should beat ourselves; an example of stern self-discipline that we must somehow follow, and God help us if we fail to do so. If *Jesus* could do it, the implication seems to be, then *we* can too. Yet is that really the point being made? The temptation Jesus faced was to take the easy path rather than the hard, to fit in with the way of the world instead of walking the way of the cross. It is his refusal to do so that gives us reason to hope and rejoice despite our faults. He took the road of costly self-sacrifice, the route that led to death, not because we deserve his mercy but because we don't, because he loves us as we are, warts and all. Lent speaks of the God who longs not to punish but to forgive.

Music *Desert waters (Music for Lent, Holy Week and Easter)* Keith Duke

Reading Matthew 4:1–11

Meditation of the devil

'Go on,' I told him,
'throw yourself off!
God's angels will save you –
you know it's true.'
And for a wonderful moment
I actually thought it might work –
my efforts succeed at last.
All right, so I'd tried twice already,
appealing first to hunger,
then to greed,
but those were bodged attempts,
crude and clumsy,
destined to fail from the start.
This time I'd learnt from my mistakes
got the measure of my man,
and was ready to pounce.
You see, it wasn't plenty he was after,

nor power,
nor personal gain at all,
but to serve *God,*
putting *him* first and self second,
the good of others before his own,
and, disturbingly, he was serious,
resolved to stay true whatever the cost.
I knew he could do it,
but did *he*? –
that was the question.
He was human, remember,
as prone as the rest of you
to that niggling voice of doubt,
and who better than *me* to oblige!
'So you're God's Son,' I murmured.
'Yes, of course.'
'But why not be sure?
Why lean on faith when proof is in your grasp?'
And then,
to clinch it all,
a whispered aside:
'God doesn't want you to die.'
Only of course, God *did,*
and somehow, even then, Jesus understood,
ready to take him on trust and give his all.
Well, that was it,
no point trying any more,
for if *that* wouldn't crack him,
nothing would.
He'd resisted temptation,
refusing to yield,
and, to cap it all,
as I sloped off,
those angels I'd promised appeared by his side,
not to *save* him,
but to help him stay true,
so that, far from *cheating* death,
he would *beat* it,
once and for all.

Silence

Prayer Lord Jesus Christ,
we praise you for your love, courage and commitment
in walking the way of the cross.
We thank you that,
though you had good reason to succumb to temptation,
you stood firm to the end,
refusing to compromise your calling.
Forgive our weakness
that stands in such contrast to your strength –
the ease with which we are led astray,
the readiness with which we dilute our principles,
the excuses with which we shut out your voice,
preferring, instead, our own.
Help us to follow you more faithfully,
not in any attempt to earn your love,
but simply to respond to it,
celebrating the grace that reconciles us with you,
despite our many faults and failings.
Amen.

Hymn Seek ye first

Comment So much of Lent points in the direction of Holy Week; in particular, to the suffering and death of Christ. But, as our next reading reminds us, we need also in this season to look beyond that to the good news of Easter, for in the story of Lazarus is a foreshadowing of that world-changing event to come. Here, as then, a body is laid in a tomb. Here, as then, there is sorrow in the presence of death. Here, as then, it looks like the end of chapter. But also, here as then, there are new beginnings as the tomb is opened and Lazarus is raised to life. It's not yet resurrection in the sense of Easter and the promise of eternity given by Jesus to his followers, but it's a reminder nonetheless that Jesus is stronger even than death. That truth colours and transforms not just one but all of the Christian seasons.

Music *Resurrection song (Sacred Pathway)* Keith Duke

Reading John 11:1–45

Meditation of Lazarus

He called me out of the tomb,
his words somehow reaching into the darkness
and restoring life.
One moment, oblivion –
and the next I was up on my feet,
shuffling out of the tomb.
One moment, trussed up like a chicken,
mummified before my time,
and the next scratching my head in bewilderment,
baffled by the look on their faces.
They thought me a ghost,
gazing in astonishment and reaching out in disbelief.
I'd been dead,
and was alive again,
really alive –
not just existing as I'd done previously,
but enthused with a joy such as I'd never known before,
set free not just from my grave clothes
but from everything that had held me captive,
denying and destroying life.
I'll die eventually, of course,
just like anyone else,
but he summoned me from the grave,
defeating the power of death,
and I know now that in the fullness of time,
he's able to do the same again and more besides,
not just for me
but for all.

Silence

Prayer

Eternal God,
thank you for the hope you give us –
a hope that will not disappoint.
Thank you for the knowledge that
though this life must come to an end –
bringing with it the trauma of bereavement,
the anguish of losing loved ones,
the bleak awareness of our own mortality –
we are able, finally, to face death
not with despair, fear or resignation,
but in quiet confidence

assured that it is a stepping stone to new beginnings,
the start of a fresh chapter –
a pathway into your kingdom
and the joy of everlasting life,
lived with you and all your people for evermore.
Amen.

Hymn In heavenly love abiding

Comment 'Transfiguration' – it's a strange word, isn't it, sounding very odd to modern ears. Yet it's not half as odd as the incident it relates to; the awesome experience of Jesus and the apostles up on the mountaintop. Curious this may be, but it's important nonetheless, for it reminds us how even those closest to Jesus wrestled before his death with a curious mixture of faith and understanding, glimpsing something of his glory yet only a fraction of the whole. This day reminds us that faith is about paradox; that Jesus was God yet man, sovereign yet servant, the giver of life through suffering death. Only if we understand the unity in this tension will we grasp the true meaning of who he was, what he did, and what he continues to do.

Music *The love of God/The gate of glory (Music for Lent, Holy Week and Easter)* Keith Duke

Reading Matthew 17:1–9

Meditation of the Apostle James

We saw him that day as never before,
literally in a new light,
glimpsing for the first time just who and what he was.
He'd been simply one of *us* until then,
special, yes,
amazing even,
but essentially a friend,
a teacher,
a person like you and me.
Yet up there on the mountaintop all that changed,
for there was more –
much more –
our eyes opened to new horizons,

the awesome, astonishing truth.
Don't ask for details –
it's all a blur –
but one moment we were catching our breath
from the climb
and the next gasping in wonder;
one moment passing the time of day
and the next prostrate in worship,
for suddenly he was transformed before us,
his clothes white as white,
his face radiant,
the world bathed in light.
It was like a divine Yes,
as though everything had been leading up
to that moment,
and as if to confirm it,
Moses and Elijah appeared by his side,
the bringer of the Law and greatest of the prophets
joining in joyful welcome
The moment passed, of course, as all do,
and after the heights of the mountain
came the depths of the valley,
descent into the shadow of death.
But though darkness came and night fell,
through a kiss, a cross and a tomb,
we looked forward in faith to the dawn,
for we had seen God's glory,
the shining of his Son,
light that would rise again.

Silence

Prayer Lord Jesus Christ,
we delight in the fact that you walked on our earth,
sharing our humanity,
being one with us,
but we can forget sometimes that,
just as you were with God in the beginning
so you are with him now,
enthroned on high,
and that, throughout your life and ministry,
you made him known,

revealing his wonder and glory
to all who had eyes to see and ears to hear.
Save us from ever reducing the divine to our level,
such that our worship becomes cosy,
comfortable
and complacent.
Help us, instead,
to discern the splendour of the godhead,
the awesomeness of who and what you are,
and thus to come before you in awe and reverence,
rejoicing at the privilege of entering your presence,
receiving your love
and sharing your life.
Amen.

Hymn The king of love my shepherd is

Closing prayer We have drawn aside from the world, Lord;
help us now to return and live out our faith within it.
We have heard your word;
help us now to put it into practice.
We have stood in your presence;
help us now to make you known.
We have received your mercy;
help us now to forgive others.
We have heard again your call;
help us now to answer.
We have offered our worship;
help us now to praise you in our daily lives.
Go with us,
and help us to walk faithfully with *you*.
Amen.

Lent (2)

Suggested visual material

Jesus of Nazareth 2
Jesus of Nazareth 3
Jesus of Nazareth 4
The Life of Christ II

Introduction

A time to reflect, to take stock of where we are and where we are going, to examine ourselves and our progress in faith, to be still in the presence of God – perhaps this idea, more than any, sums up the true significance of Lent and the opportunity it presents in terms of Christian discipleship. In the busy routine of life, with its many pressures and responsibilities, we all need a few moments set aside in order to recharge our batteries and revitalise our commitment, to get our bearings in the ongoing journey of discipleship. God can so easily be crowded out as we hurry from one thing to the next, desperate to squeeze the most out of the unforgiving minute, but however pressing our concerns may be, none can be more important than drawing on him to nourish and nurture our faith. Neglect that, and we will find all our striving gets us nowhere, leaving instead an emptiness that cannot be filled. In this service, then, we make time to pause and ponder; to reflect on what Jesus meant to those privileged to be touched directly by his ministry, and what he continues to mean for us today.

Opening prayer

Living God,
we consecrate this service to you,
asking you to speak through all that we will share.
Quieten our minds and still our souls,
so that we may recognise your presence
and discern more fully your guidance.
Help us to commit not just these few moments to you
but our whole selves,
putting you at the centre of our lives
rather than relegating you to the margins.
Teach us that communion with you is the cornerstone

upon which all else is built,
the foundation of faith and discipleship.
Just as *you* always have time for *us*,
teach *us* to make time for *you*.
Amen.

Hymn Be still, for the presence of the Lord

Comment Baptising the Messiah – for John the Baptist that was surely the highlight of his ministry, the pinnacle of his prophetic career. Yet was the euphoria he must have felt dampened by what happened next? For instead of launching straightaway into his own ministry, Jesus vanished into the wilderness, nothing more being heard of him for a time afterwards. Was John puzzled, confused, even troubled by this unexpected development? It's a possibility worth exploring.

Music *Danse profane (Danses sacrée et profane)* Debussy

Reading Mark 1:9–15

Meditation of John the Baptist

What was he doing,
going off into the wilderness like that?
I'd baptised him just hours earlier,
seen God's blessing rest upon him –
confirmation, if any were needed,
that he was the one sent from God,
the Messiah for whom we longed –
and I'd expected him to hit the ground running:
to rally support,
energise the crowds,
lay claim at once to his throne.
But instead, he disappeared,
heading off into the hills,
and no sight or sound of him for weeks to come.
Was he having second thoughts, I wondered?
Was the job too much for him?
Or had I simply misunderstood my man?
I watched . . .
and I waited . . .

torn between a mixture of dread and hope,
until, at last, word came that he was healing the sick,
saving the lost,
proclaiming the dawn of God's kingdom.
Suddenly I understood.
He'd needed to experience
the wasteland of temptation
before he was ready to transform
the desert of human life.
He'd faced the stark choice of self or others,
of taking the easy or hard way,
and he'd resolved to give his all.
Quite simply, but wonderfully,
he'd entered the wilderness to lead us out!

Silence

Prayer Lord Jesus Christ,
when we wrestle with temptation,
struggling to overcome the voice within
that seeks to lead us astray,
remind us that we are not left to face it alone.
When we fall to temptation,
giving in yet again to what we know to be wrong,
compromising our convictions,
denying your love,
betraying our calling,
remind us that you understand.
When we despair of ourselves,
frustrated at our weakness,
our lack of faith,
our fragile commitment
and our feeble resolve,
remind us that we are not forgotten.
Teach us that you too faced temptation,
and overcame it,
that you turned your back
on the rewards of this world
so that we might rejoice in the riches
of your kingdom.
Help us to receive your generous forgiveness
and to walk your way more faithfully,

not in *our* strength,
but in *yours*.
Amen.

Hymn Lord, we turn to you for mercy

Comment Ask the average Christian which of the apostles they warm to most and they'll probably come up with Peter. It's not just because he's the most often mentioned and therefore the one we know most about. It's because he comes across as completely human; as weak, flawed and prone to error as you and me. He meant well, that much is obvious, but time and again he put his foot in it, made the wrong call, let himself down. And we can relate to that, for most of us are all too aware of our own shortcomings in discipleship. Peter had to learn some hard and painful lessons on his personal journey of faith, and – as our next reading and meditation remind us – to his eternal credit, he did just that.

Music *Have mercy, Lord (St Matthew's Passion)* J. S. Bach

Reading Mark 8:31–38

Meditation of Peter

Did those words of his hurt, you ask?
Well yes, of course they did.
It's not every day someone calls you Satan.
And to be labelled such by your closest friend,
one you love and admire beyond all others –
understandably it leaves you shaken.
But let's be clear,
I deserved it, a hundred per cent,
for I should have known better.
It wasn't like he'd said anything new
in warning us he must die.
He'd been utterly open about it from the start,
clear that he came not to lord it over us
as the Romans did,
but to serve through sacrifice,
winning glory through humility,
triumph through defeat,
life through death.

Yet, I still couldn't get my head round that;
still saw success through human eyes
rather than divine.
'You *can't* die!' I told him.
'You *mustn't*!'
Understandable, perhaps,
but wrong –
hideously, hopelessly wrong.
For if he didn't surrender his life,
choosing instead to serve self rather than others,
there would be no gospel to proclaim,
no Messiah to set us free.
I may have meant well,
but that wasn't enough,
the road to hell, as they say,
being paved with good intentions.
I wanted joy without sorrow,
pleasure without pain,
answers that asked nothing of *him*
and still less of *me*,
and he helped me to realise that,
for his kingdom to come,
there must necessarily be cost:
a price *he* would pay,
for us *all*.

Silence

Prayer Lord Jesus Christ,
we struggle to come to terms with your way,
for it cuts across the norms and expectations
of this world.
We resist the idea of surrendering all,
of losing our life in order to find it.
Like Peter, confronted by the stark reality of the cross,
we find ourselves asking:
isn't there a less costly, less demanding path?
Teach us the values of your kingdom,
where the last are first and the least greatest.
Teach us the meaning of love –
above all, of your love that fills the universe,
changing lives and transforming history.

Help us, then,
for all our doubts and lack of understanding,
to celebrate what you have done,
and obediently to walk your way.
Amen.

Hymn Take up thy cross, the Saviour said

Comment What must it have felt like to be one of the multitude listening to the Sermon on the Mount? The words of Jesus may be familiar and special to us now, but to those of his time they were revolutionary, radical, and must have left his hearers wondering just who was this man with the temerity to pronounce so confidently on the true meaning of their age-old Law. Would yours have been a knee-jerk reaction, automatically rejecting this presumptuous upstart, or would you have been open to the challenge he brought? After our next reading, which gives us just a flavour of what Jesus taught – we reflect on what an enlightened Pharisee, listening to Jesus' words, might have concluded about his message.

Music *Gratias (Mass in C minor)* Mozart

Reading Matthew 6:1–6

Meditation of a Pharisee

I hate to say it, but he was right,
his analysis of true worship and sacrifice spot on.
I'd fasted often
and given generously,
even going short on occasions myself,
but commendable though it all seemed,
dedicated,
devout,
it was chiefly about me,
for *my* benefit as much as any.
I'd *intended* to serve God,
and for a time thought I had,
but though I didn't exactly trumpet it,
I made quite sure others knew of my zeal in charity,
constancy in devotion,

and steadfastness in self-denial.
And there was more, besides,
for even my *unseen* acts of devotion were tarnished,
offered simply to bask in the glow
of having done my bit,
or in the expectation of material reward.
Hearing Jesus, however, brought home to me
that piety is not enough,
for God looks beneath the surface,
into the heart and mind,
assessing not only what we do but also why we do it,
the thought as well as the action,
and by that yardstick, I fear,
I was measured and found wanting.
'So what now?' I hear you ask.
Will I still fast,
still deny myself,
still give to others?
Well yes, I certainly intend to,
but out of *love* this time,
joy instead of duty,
and as to where and when,
let alone how much or what,
don't ask me that,
or at least don't expect an answer if you do,
for I've learnt that some things
are between me and him,
and are far best staying that way.

Silence

Prayer Gracious God,
give us a heart devoted to you,
a mind focused on you,
a will committed to you,
a life dedicated to your service.
May our faith, service and witness
never be a matter of routine,
offered out of a sense of duty or compulsion,
still less an empty going through the motions.
Above all,
save us from self-serving religion –

from a pseudo-discipleship
aimed at salving our conscience,
earning rewards,
seeking our own ends
or bolstering our ego.
Teach us to love you for who and what you are,
seeking your will and walking your way
for the sheer joy of doing so.
Amen.

Hymn Will you come and follow me

Comment Have you ever felt that you're furiously busy yet getting nowhere, rushing about from one thing to the next without quite ever tackling any of them properly? If so, you'll understand why Jesus urged his disciples to take a break, to draw aside for a few moments from the work he'd entrusted to them in order to spend a few moments away from it all with him. Time and space for stillness, prayer and reflection; time and space for God – our final reading and meditation highlight the importance of such times.

Music *Now is my quiet (The New Dawn)* Margaret Rizza

Reading Mark 6:30–34, 53–56

Meditation of Matthew

He was concerned for the multitude, we knew that,
for he'd ministered to them so often,
responding to the broken in body, mind and spirit,
and bringing hope and healing.
But he was equally concerned about *us* –
about our wholeness too.
We'd forgotten that in our excitement,
too focused on our new-found mission
after he sent us out to preach and teach in his name.
Some of us had travelled miles,
determined to cover the most ground,
reach the most people,
win the most converts,
each vying to outdo the other,
almost as if it were a competition.

We meant well, of course,
but, looking back, I realise it was too much about us,
and too little about him –
as though everything depended on *our* efforts,
whereas finally, of course, it was down to him.
You should have seen us when we got together again.
Like excited schoolchildren we were,
each desperate to share what we'd been up to
and to win his plaudits,
but he gently quietened us,
urging us first to get some rest and take some food.
The message was simple:
we were called to *serve*,
not run ourselves into the ground;
to minister to *others*
but also to take care of *ourselves*,
and, to do that,
we needed time and space for reflection –
time and space for God.
He didn't ram the point home,
just gently offered guidance,
and events were to prove him right,
for, before we knew it, the crowd was upon us again,
jostling,
seeking,
demanding.
We realised then, more than ever,
the wisdom of his words,
the importance of physical and spiritual refreshment.
Work for God's kingdom, certainly,
do what you can to bring it nearer,
but don't think it depends entirely on you.
Make time for yourself as well as others,
or else you'll be no use to anyone,
including him.

Silence

Prayer Loving God,
among the duties and concerns of another day,
we can so easily forget you,
failing to make time simply to be still
and to focus on your presence.
We rush from one thing to another,
and forget what's most important:
communion with you.
Even tasks undertaken in your service,
involvement in the life and work of your Church,
can suck us into a vortex of frenetic activity,
well meant,
sincerely offered,
yet ultimately drawing us away
from prayer and devotion,
from relating to you one to one.
Teach us that,
for our physical, emotional and spiritual well-being,
we need sometimes to step back from the world
and to recognise that you are God,
for if we lose sight of that,
we lose sight of everything.
Amen.

Hymn Be still and know that I am God

Closing prayer Lord Jesus Christ,
we remember how you drew aside from the crowds,
taking time out from preaching and teaching
to spend time alone with God.
Teach us that if *you* needed to do that,
then *we* need it all the more,
our faith depending on his grace to feed it
if it is to grow and flourish.
Save us from a faith that has no time
to pause and ponder –
from allowing the affairs of daily life so to dominate
that we lose sight of what really counts.
Whatever the demands upon us,
teach us to make quality time for you,
to hear your voice,
know your will

and rejoice in your gracious love,
now and for evermore.
Amen.

Lent (3)

Suggested visual material

Jesus of Nazareth 2
Jesus of Nazareth 3
Jesus of Nazareth 4
The Life of Christ II

Introduction

We are here in Lent – a season that calls us to pause and ponder, to examine ourselves, to reflect upon our call to discipleship and the nature of our faith. Through readings and reflections, hymns and prayers, we respond today to that challenge, stepping back into the events of Christ's ministry and, through exploring what they meant then, asking what they mean for us now in our continuing journey of faith.

Opening prayer

Loving God,
stir our hearts that we might worship you,
touch our hearts that we might love you,
quieten our hearts
that we might recognise your presence among us now
and be equipped to know and serve you always.
We come gladly,
praising you for grace and goodness
We come with sorrow,
acknowledging that, once again,
we have strayed from your ways like lost sheep,
ignoring your guidance and flouting your will.
Forgive us,
and in your mercy help us to start again.
Draw near,
increase our faith,
deepen our commitment
and strengthen our love
so that we might live and work for you
to the glory of your name.
Amen.

Hymn

O love, how deep, how broad, how high

Comment For many, if not most of us, Lent is about giving something up, whether it's conquering a habit or overcoming some particular vice. But, of course, that's more easily said than done, temptation proving hard to resist. It must have been equally hard for Jesus out in the wilderness, for the temptations were real yet subtle, yet though he was tempted as we are he remained without sin. Gain strength from his example and, should you fall again – as all of us almost certainly will – give thanks that through his standing firm we not only have forgiveness but the opportunity to start again.

Music *Confutatis (Requiem)* Mozart

Reading Luke 4:1–13

Meditation of the devil

I gave up eventually,
for it was futile to continue,
all my efforts a waste of time.
Try as I might,
I was never going to deflect this guy
from the straight and narrow,
even if I stayed out there in the desert for ever
I'd deployed my usual tricks –
the promise of material comfort,
earthly glory,
divine protection –
and each time he'd seen through me,
committing himself yet more firmly
to his chosen path.
So I made my exit,
discretion being the better part of valour and all that.
But don't imagine for a moment
that I'd finished with him.
Not likely!
You might have given up, perhaps,
but not me –
it's simply not my style to lose heart
at the first setback.
No, mine was more of a tactical retreat,
a temporary withdrawal to consider options,

make fresh plans,
before coming at him again.
And mark my words,
there would be opportunities again,
for you humans,
even one as unusual as him,
all have your weak spots,
places where I can prod and probe
until you finally succumb.
You think he's different?
Well, we'll see about that.
Let's wait till he's asked to choose between survival and surrender,
between looking after number one
and pursuing his ridiculous way of love and service to the very end.
Then we'll see what he's made of, won't we?
Then we'll know, one way or the other,
which of us is the stronger.

Silence

Prayer Lord Jesus Christ,
you know what it is to be tempted, just as we are,
yet, such was your closeness to God,
that you always stood firm,
resisting whatever would deflect you
from your calling.
Give us strength to withstand temptation in turn,
to say no to the siren voices that seek to lead us astray.
Help us so to know you
that we delight to walk your way,
and when we wander from your side,
through your grace draw us back.
Amen.

Hymn Forty days and forty nights

Comment The trouble with giving something up for Lent is that this season – and, indeed, faith itself – all too easily becomes about what we *don't* do rather than what we *do*. And that's not just a shame, it's a catastrophe, for it turns faith into a matter of rules and regulation – the very thing Jesus emphasised it should never be. True discipleship means active service, living a life of love that testifies unequivocally to him. Lose sight of that and we lose sight of everything.

Music *Let your beauty (Awakening in Love)* Margaret Rizza

Reading Matthew 6:1–6, 16–21

Meditation of Matthew

Are we called to a faith that doesn't show,
a commitment none can see?
It sounds like it, doesn't it,
yet he'd spoken, just moments earlier,
of letting our light shine,
our good works speaking to others of God.
It's no incognito discipleship we're called to,
a faith ashamed to own its name,
but it's no self-serving discipleship either,
speaking more of *us* than *him*.
And, believe me, that can happen,
more easily than you might think.
Those hypocrites he spoke of . . .
do you think they set out to parade their virtue?
Perhaps they do now,
but once they were probably as sincere as any,
their prayers, almsgiving and fasting
a sign of true devotion . . .
only for outward show, over the years,
to replace inner substance.
Our relationships can grow stale,
even when it comes to God,
what once was natural as breathing,
becoming artificial,
forced,
put on for appearance only.
That's what Jesus was warning against –
faith that's become a façade,

more about being seen to look the part
than anything real underneath.
Don't think about your good works,
still less display them,
or they'll be good no longer,
simply a means to an end.
Keep them between yourself and God,
a spontaneous loving response,
and then, truly, you'll give glory to him.

Silence

Prayer Keep my faith real, Lord,
fresh and alive.
Save me from it ever becoming a matter of habit
or duty,
a going though the motions
masking a lack of substance beneath.
Nurture and nourish our relationship with you,
so that our love may always remain
as natural, deep and sincere
as the day on which it first was born.
Amen.

Hymn Lord, the light of your love is shining

Comment If Lent is about withstanding temptation and deepening commitment, it has a third, equally important aspect: making time for God. Despite all the labour-saving gadgetry we enjoy today, it's said that people in our modern world live more frenetic lives than ever before, rushing here, there and everywhere. Many of us have forgotten what it means to pause and ponder; what it means, in other words, to be still in the presence of God. We may indeed be busy – or, at least, we may think we are – but, if so, we need to sort our priorities out, making time for what matters most. If God isn't important, then what is?

Music *I give my work to you, Lord (Awakening in Love)*
Margaret Rizza

Reading Luke 10:38–42

Meditation of Martha

Don't feel sorry for me,
as if I was harshly judged,
unfairly treated,
for I wasn't,
not in the slightest.
Yes, there were jobs to be done –
the meal to prepare for a start –
but Jesus was in no hurry,
and neither should I have been.
The daft thing is it was *me* who invited him round,
not Mary;
I the one initially who recognised a gap in our lives
that Jesus alone could fill.
But I allowed myself to get distracted,
led into a blind alley by tasks that,
though worthy enough in themselves,
finally counted for nothing.
Not that Jesus minded, even then.
He knew I meant well
and would listen eventually.
It was my complaints that stirred a response:
my seeking to land Mary in it,
as though she were at fault and I virtuous,
when the true error was mine.
He rebuked me for that,
if you can call it a rebuke,
but his words were patient, gentle,
explaining rather than condemning,
inviting me to pause and think again.
I'm learning to do that, slowly,
making time to stop and stare,
relax and reflect,
and I've found true rest in doing so
not just for the body but for the soul.
It doesn't come easy to me,
for I'm the fussing sort,
always on tenterhooks,
but Jesus taught me a vital lesson that day:
there's a difference between what *seems* to matter
and what *really does*.

Silence

Prayer Teach us, Lord, that,
however busy we are,
however frenetic our lifestyle,
we need time to ponder,
time for you.
Forgive us that that we relegate you
to the margins of our lives,
believing we have more important things to do,
more pressing concerns to see to.
Remind us that you hold the words of eternal life,
the answer to our inner hunger and true needs,
and so, in our list of daily priorities,
help us to put you *first*,
not *last*.
Amen.

Hymn I lift my eyes to the quiet hills

Comment We've spoken already about the forgiveness God offers us in Christ and the new beginnings he makes possible through him, and in the parable of Jesus recorded in our next reading those are wonderfully spelt out for us. Lent can sometimes come across as a bit sombre or severe, but it shouldn't because, as with every season, at its heart lies the message of God's awesome mercy and grace.

Music *Kyrie eleison (Fountain of Life)* Margaret Rizza

Reading Luke 13:1–9

Meditation of a landowner listening to Jesus

I had a fig tree once,
and, guess what:
I got rid of it.
It was just like the one in his parable,
barren,
not a hint of fruit,
so I got the gardener to cut it down
and plant another in its place.
Should I have waited perhaps?

Given it a little more time?
Maybe,
but I reckon, if I had, I'd still be twiddling my thumbs,
waiting in vain for that first crop.
We want results, don't we? –
something to show for our efforts,
and when that fails to come, patience soon wears thin,
before long, exhausted.
Not so with Jesus.
Though we fail him time and again,
he perseveres with us,
refusing to write us off.
Though we promise much yet yield nothing,
repeatedly he forgives,
always ready to offer another chance.
Is your faith as fruitful as it should be?
Mine isn't,
nowhere near –
it's barely fruitful *at all*.
Yet those words of Jesus give me heart,
for though *I* give up believing I can ever change,
he does not.

Silence

Prayer Gracious Lord,
we despair of ourselves sometimes,
for we repeatedly fail you,
stubbornly and rebelliously flouting your will.
Thank you for not giving up on us
though we feel like doing so ourselves,
for patiently and lovingly forgiving our faults
and offering us chance after chance to start again.
Help us to grow in faith, love and commitment,
so that we might finally bear fruit for you.
Amen.

Hymn Amazing grace!

Comment Lent opens by focusing on the temptation of Jesus at the start of his ministry; it closes by taking us into Holy Week and the days leading up to the cross. But, as our next reading and meditation make clear, it is not a question of promising beginnings ending in tragedy, of hope finishing in despair – anything but!

Music *Ave verum* Mozart

Reading Luke 13:31–35

Meditation of Mary Magdalene

They brought home to me, those words in Jerusalem,
just how much he cared,
for there was real sorrow in his voice,
real pain,
real anguish.
He wasn't just playing a part,
going through the motions,
as though his time on earth were some necessary evil
before he could return to heaven.
He was committed to us,
passionately concerned,
his heart aching for all to know his love,
taste his blessing,
experience his joy.
But though he longed to embrace us,
as a mother cradles her child,
a hen gathers her brood,
he compelled no one to accept –
respecting their right to refuse –
and, tragically, for many that was so,
his message and purpose passing them by.
He continued regardless,
resolute to the end,
not even hatred and rejection deflecting his love,
but though he gave his all to redeem his own,
still they would not hear.
He's risen now,
triumphant over death and exalted on high,
but don't think that means he's detached,
remote,
indifferent to our needs.

He still cares as passionately as ever –
for you,
for me,
for everyone –
more than we will ever know.
Respond . . .
and receive.

Silence

Prayer Saviour Christ,
thank you that we matter to you,
that you truly care about our welfare.
Thank you that, whatever we do,
you never stop loving us;
that however often we push you away
you reach out still,
longing to welcome us into your embrace.
Help us to understand the depth of your devotion,
and to receive the blessing you so long to give.
Amen.

Hymn Love divine, all loves excelling

Closing prayer Send us out, Lord,
strong in faith,
fervent in service
assured of your presence.
Send us out rejoicing in your mercy,
marvelling at your love,
secure in your grace.
Send us out to speak for you,
work for you,
love for you,
live for you,
in the name of Christ
who gave everything for all.
Amen.

The Opening Days of Holy Week

The Opening Days of Holy Week (1)

Suggested visual material

Jesus of Nazareth 5
The Life of Christ III
Oberammergau 1990
Man of the Cross
He Carries our Cross

Introduction

From glad 'Hosannas!' to shouts of 'Crucify!', from the joy of Palm Sunday to the sorrow of the cross – there seems such a gulf, doesn't there; such a massive shift in people's responses and the emotions associated with them? Yet, of course, the dichotomy is more apparent than real, for Jesus was welcomed as an earthly king rather than a suffering Messiah; as one who came to rule, not serve; to conquer, not die! Even at its best, the love and commitment his followers offered him was flawed, more about what they wanted from him than what he came to do. Yet, knowing all that, fully aware of our human limitations, he continued to his death, faithful to the end despite our faithlessness. That is the Lord we worship. That is the saviour we seek to honour. That is the message we celebrate, not just today but every day. Through this service let us remind ourselves afresh of the one who gave so much for us who deserve so little.

Opening prayer

Lord Jesus Christ,
we remember today the contrasting responses
to your ministry:
how some greeted you with shouts of joy
and songs of praise,
saluting you as king,
while others muttered against you,
scheming and plotting,
intent on doing you down.
We remember how 'Hosanna!' turned to 'Crucify!',
welcome to rejection;
how those who professed undying loyalty

turned tail and ran;
but we remember also how one thing stayed constant:
your selfless love for all!
Inspire us again through your awesome sacrifice,
so that we may receive you more fully into our hearts
and commit ourselves afresh to your service.
Amen.

Hymn All glory, laud and honour

Comment Coming in with a bang, going out with a whimper – in the eyes of many, that could be said to describe the last days of the life of Jesus leading up to the cross. One moment, as we noted earlier, he was accorded a positively rapturous welcome as he rode into Jerusalem, and the next moment the crowds were baying for his blood, declaring they had no other king than Caesar. It's a truly breathtaking turnaround in his fortunes, and a reader coming to the story for the first time could be forgiven for thinking that those who welcomed Jesus as their king on Palm Sunday were sadly mistaken – misguided if not deluded. Yet such a conclusion would be wrong for, as Holy Week reminds us, the betrayal, arrest and crucifixion of Christ were not some unfortunate error somehow rectified at Easter but part of God's purpose, integral to the rule and kingdom that Jesus came to bring. If we see him as sovereign yet not as servant, as raised high without also being brought low, we have altogether missed the point.

Music *Sanctus Dominus (River of Peace)* Margaret Rizza

Reading Matthew 21:1–11

Meditation of one of the crowd in Jerusalem

You should have seen the crowd that day!
All round him, they were,
rushing ahead,
pushing behind –
a seething mass surging through the city gates,
shouting themselves hoarse.
They were ecstatic,

waving palm branches in welcome
and lining the way with their coats.
'Hosanna!' they cried.
'Hosanna to the Son of David!'
'Blessed be the Lord!'
And the one at their *centre*?
A guy called Jesus apparently,
from up north in Galilee.
The name rang a bell,
for I'd heard tales of signs and wonders,
a man who healed the sick,
fed the multitude,
stilled the storm –
a prophet like none other, according to some.
But you could have fooled me,
for I saw nothing special about him,
nothing to catch the eye –
just an ordinary person,
like you and me.
Yet still they cheered,
still they chanted,
as though he were Messiah himself,
the Son of God,
a conquering king.
It's a puzzle,
for, were he that,
I'd have expected a fanfare of trumpets,
chariot of gold and royal procession,
not a man riding on a *donkey*,
but he must have something about him
to cause such a stir,
some gift to win hearts and capture minds.
I'm not sure what,
not sure how,
but I mean to find out,
for it's intriguing, isn't it?
Too intriguing to ignore.

Silence

Prayer Lord Jesus Christ,
save us from confusing the values of this world
with your own,
from seeing your heavenly rule
as one that forces itself on people –
demanding,
coercing,
imposing.
Teach us that, instead, yours is the way of love,
inviting a response –
surrendering,
liberating,
serving.
Help us, then, to deny ourselves,
in order to discover who we really are;
to be last so as to be first;
to lose our life in order to find it –
to walk the royal way of the cross.
Amen.

Hymn You are the King of Glory

Comment Actions, we say, speak louder than words, and that comes out, in two important senses, during the incident recorded in our next reading. First, because Mary, through anointing Jesus' feet with perfume, shows her love and commitment to him in a way that words alone could never do. She knows instinctively that he is reaching a critical moment in his ministry, and rather than offer him empty clichés she wants to show how special he was to her. So she pours out the costliest thing she owns: her rare and precious perfume. But, of course, unbeknown to her, her actions speak more deeply, foreshadowing an even costlier sacrifice and the way that Jesus' body will soon be anointed again, in readiness for burial. Mary's simple and impulsive action points to Christ's love for you and for all, and asks simultaneously what response you make to him.

Music *Pié Jesu* (*Requiem*) Fauré

Reading John 12:1–11

Meditation of Mary, sister of Martha and Lazarus

I'd scrimped and saved for that perfume,
for it spoke of luxury,
style,
sophistication.
It was my chance to be a lady –
to turn heads,
walk tall –
yet, having made it mine,
I gave it away in a single extravagant gesture,
an outpouring of love.
Profligate, some called it –
headstrong folly –
and yes, maybe it was over the top,
yet it seemed natural at the time,
for I wanted to offer Jesus something special –
not just any old gift
but one of real value,
speaking straight from the heart.
So I took that perfume and anointed his feet,
wiping them clean with my hair.
You should have smelt the place:
overpowering or what!
Like a brothel, I thought,
a boudoir,
a place of burial.
And that latter thought clearly struck Jesus,
for he spoke suddenly of death,
of being taken from us,
almost as though he were already a corpse
and I the embalmer.
We were shocked,
stunned,
dismissing the idea as nonsense,
but a week later he was dead,
cut down from a cross and sealed in a tomb,
anointed for burial again.
It had seemed costly, that gift of mine,
an example of self-denial,

but suddenly it felt pathetically small,
for the true sacrifice was his.
I'd offered a *little* –
he'd given his *all*.

Silence

Prayer Lord Jesus Christ,
we think we know what it means to deny ourselves,
but in reality we have little idea at all.
We content ourselves with token actions –
a hunger lunch, perhaps,
a temporary renunciation of some little luxury,
a few extra pounds given to charity –
and then we pat ourselves on the back,
as though we've achieved something special,
truly gone without.
Remind us of the immensity of *your* sacrifice –
your willingness to endure not only death,
but the weight of human evil,
in order to redeem us and bring us life.
Help us,
conscious of that awesome love,
to understand what self-denial really means,
and to put it more meaningfully into practice.
Amen.

Hymn Jesus, name above all names

Comment In chapels and churches across the country you will often find, displayed inside their pulpits, a terse message: 'Sir, we would see Jesus'. So employed, it constitutes a stern admonition to the preacher, warning them to get things right or face the consequences, but it was spoken first by Greek visitors to Jerusalem mentioned in our next reading; pilgrims who clearly had heard something of the tales of Jesus circulating in Judea and wanted to see this celebrated personage for themselves. What was he like? Where was he from? And what did he mean for them? Assuming that these Greeks stayed in Jerusalem for the rest of that week they would indeed have seen him, though in a manner that must have taken them completely by surprise, for they would have witnessed not astonishing acts of healing or wowing the crowds, but a man mocked, flogged and nailed to a cross where, utterly broken, he suffered and died. What was going on, they must have wondered? What sort of miracle worker was this? Yet, of course, it was precisely through giving his all that Christ crucified and risen was to become known not just to them but beyond; to be not merely *seen* but worshipped, served and loved across the centuries, throughout the world.

Music *'Come to me,' says the Lord (In God Alone)* Andrew Moore

Reading John 12:20–36

Meditation of Philip

Don't ask me who they were –
I didn't know them from Adam –
but they came up to me that day
with one simple request:
'Sir, we wish to see Jesus.'
And why not?
After all, they weren't alone:
everyone wanted to see Jesus!
He was the talk of the town,
requests to see him being two a penny.
At least, they were from *Jews*,
but these guys were *Greeks* –
Gentiles in other words –
so what had he to do with them?
He's *our* leader, I reckoned,
our Messiah –
go off and get your *own*.
I didn't say that, of course,
not in so many words;
just excused myself as best I could,
and sought advice from Andrew.
Yet I couldn't get them out of my head,
for they were clearly serious,
asking not through idle curiosity
but irresistibly drawn,
the tone of their voice and look in their eyes

conveying hunger,
urgency,
a yearning within.
So we told Jesus,
and he seemed unsurprised,
as though he expected nothing less;
as though a person's creed, colour, culture
doesn't matter,
for his welcome extends to all.
And, of course, so it does,
the message of Christ crucified and risen
having been taken out to the world,
proclaimed to the ends of the earth,
Jew and Gentile alike –
no strings,
no provisos,
no limits.
He was lifted up,
not on a throne as we'd assumed,
but on a cross
to draw all people to himself,
so that finally, not just a few,
but *everyone*,
could see Jesus,
and know his love for themselves.

Silence

Prayer Loving God,
deliver us from narrow horizons,
a limited vision that confines your purpose to ourselves,
our fellowship, denomination, town or country.
Save us from seeing the good news as being for a few
rather than for the many;
as concerning the Church alone
rather than the whole world.
Make known, to the ends of the earth,
your love, joy and peace,
and help us, in every way we can,
to testify to your saving and renewing grace,
through Jesus Christ our Lord.
Amen.

Hymn And can it be

Comment 'It wasn't my fault, I couldn't help it' – probably the most common excuse made by children when they're caught doing something wrong. The truth is, of course, that ninety-nine times out of a hundred they *could* help it and it *was* their fault, but though they know full well this is so, most parents are willing to forgive and forget, even if – in some way – they first have to discipline. What about Judas? Could *he* help what he did? Was it *his* fault he betrayed Jesus? Controversy has raged over that since time immemorial. On the one hand it was an act of abject treachery, the ultimate selling out of a friend. On the other, he was playing a vital part in God's purpose, paving the way for the saving death of Christ. Did Jesus exonerate Judas from blame? I doubt it. But did he condemn him? I doubt that too. For, like his Father, was not his impulse always to forgive? Consider for yourself whether the story of the betrayal is all about human sin or divine grace.

Music *Miserere nobis (Awakening in Love)* Margaret Rizza

Reading John 13:21–32

Meditation of Judas Iscariot

They looked at me mystified,
wondering where on earth I was off to,
what business I could have at such a time of night.
An errand, they assumed,
some mission for the Master,
much as when he'd sent some of the others off
to prepare the upper room
or fetch that donkey from Jerusalem.
They suspected nothing, even then –
never dreamt treachery was afoot
despite all he'd said about death and betrayal.
Gullible fools!
Not Jesus, though –
he knew the score.
And I realised, with a sudden chill,
that he'd understood all along what I was going to do;
not simply when I hatched the plan

but earlier still,
before it even entered my head.
He knew the sort of man I am –
the weaknesses deep within,
temptations I fall prey to –
and he recognised that when the chips were down,
I'd sell out to the highest bidder,
take the cash and run.
Why did he call me, I wonder, knowing that truth?
Why did he welcome me as a disciple and friend?
Yet he not only did that,
but, unless I'm much mistaken, he *loved* me too,
actually cared about my welfare
even as I walked out of that door into the darkness.
I'd expected anger, reproach, disappointment,
but there was nothing of that in the look he gave me –
only compassion, concern, even sympathy.
It was as though he was ready for the end –
that, foolish as it may seem,
he was willing to die not just for his friends,
but for his enemies;
not just for others,
but for *me*!

Silence

Prayer Lord Jesus Christ,
however much we have understood of you,
we have barely begun to grasp the scale of your grace –
the length, breadth, height and depth of your love.
Such a willingness to forgive and go on forgiving,
give and go on giving,
defies logic,
going beyond anything we could expect or hope for,
or show in turn.
Incredible though such love may seem,
teach us that it is true,
and help us to receive it with grateful hearts.
Amen.

Hymn There's a wideness in God's mercy

Closing prayer

Lord Jesus Christ,
teach us more about the way you walked;
the path of love, service, mercy and compassion.
Remind us of your openness to all;
your willingness to give and go on giving.
Remind us of your humility;
the way you invariably put others before yourself.
Help us to understand how much you surrendered,
how much you cared and continue to care,
and may that knowledge inspire us in turn
to consecrate our lives to your kingdom,
seeking always and in everything,
to know and do your will.
Amen.

The Opening Days of Holy Week (2)

Suggested visual material

Jesus of Nazareth 5
The Life of Christ III
Oberammergau 1990
Man of the Cross
He Carries our Cross

Introduction

Waiting, we say, can be the hardest part, especially when we're facing the prospect of something frightening or unpleasant about to befall us, and no doubt that was as true for Jesus as for any. He rode into Jerusalem to the acclaim of the crowds, yet he knew that just a few days later he would face a very different reception, an altogether contrasting fate. From the start of his ministry he'd lived with the knowledge that it would lead to a cross; to suffering, sorrow and death; and now the moment had arrived, the time when he would be asked to make the final sacrifice. He could so easily have turned back, putting himself before others, but he didn't; he continued instead on his chosen path to the very end. Today, we reflect on the final stages of his journey to Calvary – on the enormity of his courage, the extent of his sacrifice and the depth of his love. Remember, and give thanks.

Opening prayer

Father God,
speak again in this Holy Week of your love in Christ,
of your surrendering all for our sakes.
Speak of his faithfulness to your call,
of his selfless service and awesome sacrifice,
and help us to remember what it cost both him
and you.
Give us similar courage to give and go on giving,
love and go on loving,
so that we, like him, may be enabled to put you first,
others second,

and self last.
Meet with us now
and teach us your way,
through Jesus Christ our Lord.
Amen.

Hymn Give me joy in my heart

Comment There's a curious paradox about Holy Week. It starts in celebration, recalling the entry of Jesus into Jerusalem, and ends solemnly, even mournfully, with the remembrance of his suffering and death. Yet the joyful mood of that first Palm Sunday turned out to be a false dawn, the welcome Jesus received from the crowd proving more apparent than real, swift to dissipate once expectations were not met, whereas apparent defeat on the cross proved in reality the greatest of victories, a death that brings life to all. What did the apostles make of the palm-waving multitude? Were they carried along by the euphoria of the moment, or were they already starting to look deeper?

Music *Praise his holy name/Glory to the high King (Music for Lent, Holy Week and Easter)* Keith Duke

Reading John 12:12–16

Meditation of Simon the zealot

I think they've got it,
finally understood who Jesus is,
for look at the welcome they're giving him:
the joy in their faces,
laughter in their eyes.
They're tearing down palm branches
in their excitement,
shouting themselves hoarse:
'Hosanna!
Blessed is the one who comes in the name
of the Lord!'
They surely realise at last that he's the Messiah,
the one sent by God to redeem his people.
Or do they?
For what is it they're calling him now:

the King of Israel.
That would have been music to my ears
not so long ago,
for it's what I longed to see:
a ruler coming to drive out the Romans,
to restore our earthly fortunes,
to establish a new era of plenty and prosperity –
with our people at the centre –
and God's kingdom here on earth.
But having walked and talked with Jesus,
having heard his message
and seen the difference he alone can bring,
I realise now that what we need is a change
not to the regime or system,
but to people's lives,
to who and what we are.
That's where he wants to reign:
in human hearts rather than on an earthly throne.
Have they understood that?
Have *any* of us?
They're welcoming him with open arms,
proclaiming their devotion,
but if he fails to deliver what they want
will their commitment hold,
their allegiance stay true?
Will they still salute him as king
if his kingdom's not of this world?
Time, I suppose, will tell.

Silence

Prayer Lord Jesus Christ,
teach us what it means to honour you,
to enthrone you in our lives.
Help us to understand that true commitment
involves more than declaring our loyalty,
however sincere that may be;
more than homage offered with our lips,
however eloquent it may sound.
Teach us to acclaim you from the heart
with lives consecrated to your service,
seeking your will and walking your way,

so that we may truly acknowledge you as Lord
and work more effectively for the growth
of your kingdom,
on earth as it is in heaven.
Amen.

Hymn What kind of greatness

Comment If Lazarus had the spotlight in John chapter 11, being astonishingly raised to life, in chapter 12 that honour moves to his sister Mary as she impulsively anoints Jesus' feet with her hair in a spontaneous gesture of love. Yet there's a third family member involved in the story, albeit passing almost unnoticed as she unobtrusively gets on with her work behind the scenes. Martha's may have been a less eye-catching ministry than her sister's, but it was just as sincere and equally valuable.

Music *I give my work to you, Lord (Awakening in Love)*
Margaret Rizza

Reading John 12:1–11

Meditation of Martha

What's that you say?
Still serving at tables?
But of course! –
wasn't that the least I could do?
Jesus had raised my brother, remember –
somehow brought him out of the tomb,
just weeks earlier,
alive and well,
when his body should,
by rights, have been rotting into dust.
The resurrection and the life, Jesus called himself,
and I'd seen for myself it was true,
the power of the grave defeated,
death put to flight.
No words could sum up how we felt,
for, through his awesome power,
he'd transformed our world,
turning darkness to light,

despair to hope,
sorrow to joy –
and we couldn't thank him enough.
But I had to *try*,
had to show him in some way how grateful I was.
So yes, I was serving again,
glad to play my part in the way I knew best.
But that's not the half of it,
for I'm resolved also to offer service of a different sort –
to walk his way and give him, as best I can,
my love,
my life,
my all.

Silence

Prayer Loving God,
speak to us again of the new life you offer,
new beginnings in Christ.
Speak of the fresh start you daily make possible –
the opportunity to put the past behind us
and to set out again,
the slate wiped clean,
the future open.
Speak of life beyond the grave,
eternal,
lived for ever with you,
unlike anything we can know now or ever imagine.
Remind us of your renewing, redeeming power,
and help us to respond in grateful service
and joyful praise,
through Jesus Christ our Lord.
Amen.

Hymn I know that my redeemer lives

Comment A red rag to a bull – that's what Jesus' actions in the Temple must have seemed like to his followers as he stormed through its precincts, overturning the stalls of those trading there. What was he thinking of? Surely he knew that the religious establishment was already out to get him, and that provocation such as this would only increase their hostility. So why court controversy? Why deliberately cause offence and hasten his own demise? What was so important to Jesus that he felt it necessary to make a stand, no matter what the cost?

Music *The ride of the Valkyries* Wagner

Reading John 2:13–22

Meditation of Nathanael

Why was he so annoyed, we wondered?
All right, so those money-changers and the like
were charging top whack,
but there was nothing new in that –
any trader would do the same.
Business is business, as they say –
we all have to make a living.
Yet, as we came eventually to realise,
it wasn't the prices Jesus objected to,
nor the idea of selling goods in God's house;
it went much deeper than that,
to the very heart of our faith.
He was challenging the whole system,
the idea that God's pardon depends
on anything we might do.
No, he said,
that's not how it works:
God forgives because it's in his nature to do so,
because he simply can't help loving,
our part being simply to respond and receive.
No need for sacrifices,
whether doves, pigeons or anything else.
Whatever was asked for, *he* would do on our behalf.
Faith, in his eyes,
is as extraordinary and simple as that.
Yet there in the Temple people were expected
not only to perform the required ritual
but to pay for the privilege of doing so,
as though God's favour can be bought and sold.
Those traders were stunned, I can tell you,
when he stormed in
and overturned their tables like that,
but not half as stunned as we were

when we realised what he was getting at:
that the whole Law is summed up
by the command to love,
for we'd been brought up to believe
that following it to the letter is vital –
the key to salvation.
He showed us instead a better way,
too wonderful for words.
We can't earn God's blessing,
still less deserve it.
It's his gift,
generous beyond measure,
offered freely to all,
depending not on anything we might do
but entirely on what *he* has *done*!

Silence

Prayer Almighty God, forgive us,
for we are false and faithless in so much.
Through ignorance,
weakness
or wilful disobedience
we abandon your way,
resisting and rejecting your guidance.
We lose sight of what you really want
and of what you offer to all –
a life lived in the light of your love –
turning faith instead into outward show,
a matter of observing rules and regulations
rather than of enjoying a right relationship with you.
In your great mercy,
show us the error of our ways,
and teach us joyfully to receive the blessings
you long to lavish upon us,
through Jesus Christ our Lord.
Amen.

Hymn Come, let us sing of a wonderful love

Comment If Holy Week points to one thing in particular, it is surely sacrifice – Christ's offering of himself on the cross. For three years his life and ministry had been leading up to this point: the moment when he would give his all for the sake of the world. He'd understood that cost from the beginning, but as the moment of truth drew near so the immensity of what was being asked of him hit home. But he continued nonetheless, refusing to be deflected from his chosen path. Far less is asked of us, but there are times when we too must be ready to deny ourselves, to look beyond this world to the things of heaven. Have you understood how much Jesus gave for you? And are you ready to give him something back in return?

Music *Take my life, Lord (Fire of Love)* Margaret Rizza

Reading John 12:20–33

Meditation of Andrew

'Hate their life in this world'?
What does he mean by that?
It sounds so negative,
hardly a great advert for Christianity –
as though the main criterion for following Jesus
is to be so thoroughly disenchanted
that you want to end it all!
He can't mean that, surely,
and I don't think he does,
for he's spoken repeatedly of the joy he brings,
the blessings he wants to bestow,
not just in some distant future,
but here and now.
I don't hate life in this world, that's for sure,
but I *do* hate certain aspects:
those things that wound, damage and destroy,
scarring relationships
and demeaning people as objects to be used,
exploited,
ignored;
and yes, I hate my own culpability
in its hurt and heartache,
for none of us are whiter than white,

untarnished by such faults.
Is this what Jesus had in mind?
That we must renounce this life if it leads us astray?
That we must be ready to make sacrifices,
even perhaps the greatest sacrifice of all,
in order to confront what we know to be wrong
and make a stand for good?
I can make sense of that,
strive towards it,
though I can't help feeling it's an ideal,
always out of reach,
for who among us would utterly renounce self
for the sake of others,
surrendering all for their sake?
It would take incredible courage,
unparalleled love.
Could anyone, I wonder –
even Jesus –
show devotion such as that?

Silence

Prayer God of all,
give us a proper perspective on life.
Help us to celebrate the good things you have given –
to rejoice in the beauty of this world
and the blessings you daily shower upon us.
But help us also
to grieve over whatever scars your creation,
denying your love and thwarting your purpose.
Teach us to stand up against such things,
irrespective of the cost to us,
recognising that true fulfilment
and our ultimate destiny
lie not here on earth but in your eternal kingdom,
where, by your grace, we will savour life indeed
for evermore.
Amen.

Hymn May the mind of Christ my Saviour

Comment 'Make way', run the words of a popular modern hymn: 'make way, for the King of kings . . . and let his kingdom in.' It's a statement of faith and outpouring of praise, looking forward to the time when Christ will finally be all in all. But, of course, the crowds in Jerusalem did not finally make way, or acknowledge him as king. Instead, they turned against him and called for his death, then stood watching him die. The glory of Jesus was to prove very different to that of this world, displayed not on a throne but on a cross. Many of his followers were to tread a similar path, giving their lives in his service, paying the ultimate price. Holy Week brings the challenge: how much does our faith mean to us? What, if anything, are we ready to surrender for the cause of Christ?

Music *In Paradisum (Requiem)* Fauré

Reading Mark 10:35–45

Meditation of James and John

James We *did* know what we were asking,
or at least we thought we did.
John We wanted a share of the spoils,
to be identified with Jesus,
when he came into his kingdom,
as his right-hand men,
his loyal followers,
sharing in the limelight,
basking in his glory.
James Only that's not what his glory meant.
John We hadn't fathomed it at all,
both of us still thinking in human terms:
the approbation of this world.
James And we couldn't have been more wrong,
for the crown he would wear
was one of thorns,
his lifting up to be on a cross
and his victory to be won through death.

John Would we have asked to share that glory
had we known what it involved?

James Would we have taken the way of service
and sacrifice,
of costly commitment?

John I don't think so,
for though we'd followed Jesus for years,
we'd still barely grasped
what he'd come to do.

James I tell you what though,
we grasped it later,
for we saw him suffer,
watched him die,
his life freely offered as a ransom for many.

John He's enthroned now, of course,
but his kingdom is in heaven,
not on earth,
and he, the King of kings and Lord of lords,
rules there as servant,
the one who surrendered all to make us his.

James It's my turn now to take up my cross,
and for me that's not just a figure of speech;
it's meant literally,
for I too now must give everything.
I asked for glory,
and I've got it,
though not of this world.
It's been an honour, Lord, to serve.

Silence

Prayer Lord Jesus Christ,
we try to see beyond this world,
but we struggle to do so,
for the here and now is what we know best,
the context in which we play out our daily lives.
Though we strive to do otherwise,
automatically we assess things
from a human point of view,
from what popular opinion counts as success.
Help us instead to grasp the values of your kingdom,
in which defeat is victory,

the last are first,
the weak are strong
and death brings life –
to recognise that glory, as you understand it,
is not about lording it over others
but about selfless service,
about giving rather than receiving,
a cross instead of a crown.
If we would share you glory,
teach us first what it truly means.
Amen.

Hymn You laid aside your majesty

Closing prayer Lord Jesus Christ,
inspire us through your dedication,
your willingness to take the costly path of sacrifice
in order to make us whole.
Though we will always fall short,
give us something of your courage and commitment,
your selfless love for all.
Keep our eyes,
like yours,
fixed on the joy set before us,
the things you have kept for us in heaven,
so that we may walk faithfully in your footsteps,
running the race with perseverance
to our journey's end.
Amen.

The Opening Days of Holy Week (3)

Suggested visual material

Jesus of Nazareth 5
The Life of Christ III
Oberammergau 1990
Man of the Cross
He Carries our Cross

Introduction

One week, they say, is a long time in politics, which is another way of saying that popular opinion, and hence the fate of politicians, can ebb and flow with almost frightening speed. The same could be said – with yet more truth – of the period spanning Palm Sunday to Easter Day, for that week, above all others, was one of contrasting emotions, fluctuating fortunes, the tide turning and turning again. In this service we are going to focus on but a few aspects of that astonishing time, reflecting from the perspective of Judas Iscariot, Mary (the sister of Martha and Lazarus) and one of the priests in the Jerusalem Temple on what Jesus went through, what he did and what he accomplished through the cross. As we attempt to stand for a moment in their shoes, let us consider afresh the wonder of what Christ has done for us, and for all.

Prayer

Eternal God,
in this Holy Week
we remember how Jesus was welcomed as a king,
yet condemned as a criminal;
greeted with acclaim,
yet rejected with abuse;
saluted as a saviour,
yet mocked on a cross.
We marvel at how you turned weakness to strength,
defeat to victory,
sorrow to joy
and darkness to light,
overturning the expectations of this world.

Receive our praise,
and, in the ups and down of life,
speak to us of your eternal purpose
and transforming power;
of your love that will never be defeated,
whatever it may face.
Help us to glimpse more fully
the nature of your kingdom
so that we may worship you now
and serve you always.
Amen.

Hymn Christ triumphant

Comment If there's one lesson that should have emerged from the very first Palm Sunday, when Jesus rode into Jerusalem to the welcome of the crowds, it should surely have been that God's values are different from our own and his kingdom nothing like those of this world. Jesus came as king yet in obvious humility, seated not on some mighty charger but on a donkey. He came quietly, accepting the welcome of the crowd yet not milking it, still less seeking to whip up some frenzy of expectation. The one who was the greatest of all came as the least, seeking to serve rather than be served. Yet, as our next reading reminds us, not even his disciples had begun to grasp that all-important truth; not even they had any real inkling of who he was, what he came to do, or the kingdom he came to bring.

Music *Osanna in excelsis* J. S. Bach

Reading Luke 19:28–40

Meditation of Simon the zealot

I feel so guilty,
so ashamed.
Having watched him ride into Jerusalem
humble and seated on a donkey,
we argued among ourselves
just days afterwards,
over which of us was the greatest.

Despite everything he'd said,
everything he'd done,
everything he was,
we hadn't learnt a thing –
still measuring worth and success
in terms of this world.
And while we squabbled,
there he was –
the Lord of all –
preparing for death on a cross.
How different he was from your typical king,
lording it over his subjects,
power and authority jealously guarded
and all too often abused.
He ruled through consent,
governed through service –
a king like no other,
least yet greatest of all.
Have you grasped better than we did
what that means?
Have you learnt to follow his example:
to serve *him* rather than self?
Ask yourself, as we had to that day:
which kingdom's values you live by:
those of this world
or the next?

Silence

Prayer King of kings, yet servant of all,
we worship you.
Lord of lords, yet broken for all,
we praise you.
Giver of life, yet dying for all,
we honour you.
Ruler on high, yet least of all,
we acclaim you.
Crucified king,
teach us what it means to love you,
serve you,
acknowledge you,
proclaim you,

in thought and word and deed.
Amen.

Hymn Meekness and majesty

Comment Holy Week is not a time simply for remembering, as though it is merely a reminder of the last days of Jesus' life and ministry before he faced the stark horror of the cross, a record of the bald facts concerning that fateful week. It is also a time for responding, for asking what Jesus' suffering and death mean for you and me today, what he did for each of us individually, and what that asks of us in turn. For Mary, sister of Martha and Lazarus, the need to offer her love, loyalty, service and sacrifice was obvious even before events unfolded in all their awfulness. In Jesus she had found someone special, someone who brought answers to questions and needs deep within, and instinctively she wanted to give something back to express how much that meant.

Music *Everything's all right (Jesus Christ Superstar)*
Andrew Lloyd Webber and Tim Rice

Reading John 12:1–11

Meditation of Mary, sister of Martha and Lazarus

My sister calls me complacent,
lazy even,
and she has a point,
for too often I leave her doing the work
while I swan around doing nothing.
Yet, funnily enough, she admires me,
because I'm able to stop and stare,
to appreciate the special things in life,
and to let it show how much they mean to me.
She finds that hard, you see,
for always in the back of her mind
there are those jobs to do –
so many distractions,
so much more to do,
so much else to think of.
She's somewhat shy, as well.

Not repressed, or anything like that,
but inhibited enough to want to hide her feelings,
keep them hidden from the public eye.
So when Jesus came round that day,
she was serving, just as before,
while I ostentatiously savoured the moment,
anointing his feet with oil.
I couldn't help myself,
for I saw Jesus there –
so good,
so caring,
so vulnerable –
and I wanted to show him that,
even if the world was turning against him,
I loved him as much as ever
in a way I've loved no one else before.
Judas was furious about it,
and even the others raised an eyebrow,
but not Martha this time:
she'd learnt from her rebuke before.
Don't think I was better than her,
more sincere or devoted.
I showed what he meant to me
through an extravagant gesture of love,
she through faithful service.
It's not how you respond that matters,
as though one way's superior to another.
It's whether you respond at all.

Silence

Prayer Lord Jesus Christ,
we want to express our love for you,
our gratitude,
our commitment to your cause,
but we hold back,
afraid of what others may think
or unsure how best to respond.
Teach us that nothing is set in stone;
that there is no right way we must rigidly follow.
Help us simply and in our own way
to pour out what we feel,

and to do so from the heart.
Amen.

Hymn Father, we love you

Comment One of the most striking features of the time leading up to the death of Jesus is how little everyone concerned grasped what was going on. The crowds still thought he was coming to lead a rebellion against the hated legions of Rome; the apostles still thought when he spoke of suffering and death that he must be speaking figuratively, being certain to escape when the moment of truth finally came; and his enemies still thought his fate was in their hands, as though *they* rather than God were in control of events. Our next reading and meditation pick up on that tapestry of misunderstanding. As Jesus continues to preach and teach to the crowds that have gathered around him, he explains to those with ears to hear and eyes to see exactly why he has come and what lies in store for him, but the true meaning of his words, as so often before, simply passes his listeners by.

Music *Behold the Lamb of God (Messiah)* Handel

Reading John 12:20–36

Meditation of a priest listening to Jesus

What was he on about:
'the Son of Man must be lifted up'?
Listen, we know our Scriptures,
and if Jesus had understood them half as well
he'd have avoided such a howler,
for the Son of Man will come *down*,
not go *up*!
He's to descend from on high,
sent to defeat our enemies,
take up his throne
and establish God's kingdom.
So what Jesus had in mind, heaven only knows!
It wasn't his only mistake, either,
for apparently he believed *he* was that promised one,
the answer to all our prayers,

bringing life and light to the world.
Well, we soon put a stop to that,
carting him off before Pilate
who laid not just such talk to rest,
but Jesus as well.
Funnily enough though, he *was* lifted up in a way:
nailed to a cross,
and, more strange still,
his followers claim it was part of his plan,
his way of saving us all.
They actually worship him, you know –
claim he's risen,
ascended,
if you like, lifted up *again*!
Well, more fool them,
for I saw Jesus squirm,
watched him suffer and die,
and, believe me, there was nothing glorious about it,
nothing to suggest a king and a crown.
Let them glory in a cross if they want to,
extol a broken, crucified Lord.
It will never catch on.

Silence

Prayer Thank you, Lord, for the message of the cross,
an offence to some,
nonsense to others,
but to us the power and wisdom of God.
Thank you for the awesome truth of which it speaks:
the love, forgiveness and new life you made possible
through surrendering there your all.
For the way your cross has spoken across the years
and continues still so powerfully to speak,
receive our praise.
Amen.

Hymn Lift high the cross

Closing prayer

Go with us now, Lord, into our topsy-turvy world,
and amid all its highs and lows,
joys and sorrows,
help us to trust in your kingdom,
and work to bring it closer.
Go with us in the rollercoaster of life,
and whatever our hopes or fears
triumphs or tragedies,
help us to recognise your presence by our sides.
Go with us in the days ahead,
whatever they may bring,
and despite our flawed and fickle faith,
with all its limitations,
help us to live and work for you,
to your praise and glory.
Amen.

Maundy Thursday

Maundy Thursday (1)

Suggested visual material

Jesus of Nazareth 5
The Life of Christ III
Bread and Wine
Oberammergau 1990
Man of the Cross
He Carries our Cross

Introduction

'Amazing grace, how sweet the sound, that saved a wretch like me!' – so wrote the one-time sea captain and slave trader John Newton in what has become one of the most celebrated hymns of all time. And there are surely few days of the Christian year that testify more eloquently to the grace of which he speaks than that which we celebrate today: Maundy Thursday. On the one hand, it highlights human faithlessness writ large. There's Judas Iscariot, betraying his friend Jesus in the garden of Gethsemane with a kiss. Then there's Peter who, put on the spot concerning his allegiance, denies all knowledge of the man who just hours earlier he'd proclaimed his readiness to die for. And finally there are the remaining apostles who, to a man, turn tail and run when the heat is on. What a miserable bunch they appear to be, and what a bleak future they seemingly portend for any continuation of the life and ministry of their Master. Yet, of course, this day speaks also of Christ's incomparable faith*ful*ness – a passionate commitment not just to his disciples but to all who would follow him, then, now and beyond, despite the feeble faith and callow commitment we may show. If this day reminds us more than any other of how little we deserve, it speaks also of how much God was willing to give. Amazing grace indeed!

Opening prayer

Saviour Christ,
we are reminded today
of how one of your disciples betrayed you,
and we come conscious that, in our own way,
we too also betray you,
through rejecting your guidance,
disobeying your will,
preferring the way of the world to yours.
We are reminded today
of how one of your closest friends denied you,
and we come conscious that we deny you too,
through hiding our allegiance,
through faithless discipleship,
through the way we live and fail to live.
We are reminded today
of how your followers abandoned you,
and we come conscious that we also do the same,
forsaking your way,
compromising our convictions,
hiding our allegiance –
forgetting even that you are there.
Lord,
we come to you in all our weakness,
with all our faults,
but we come also knowing that you went to the cross
for people such as us,
dying to bring us life.
Teach us to open our hearts to you,
rejoicing that you were broken to make us whole.
Amen.

Hymn Christ triumphant

Comment Think of Jesus on the night of his betrayal and arrest, and the picture that will almost certainly spring to mind is of him praying in anguish, imploring God if possible to find another way. John's Gospel, however, gives us a rather different picture. He portrays Jesus praying not in the garden of Gethsemane but in the upper room, and, as we will see, his concern was not for himself but for others, like you and me.

Music *Father, may they be one (In God Alone)* Andrew Moore

Reading John 17:1–11

Meditation of the Apostle James

You should have heard his words,
that night in the upper room
before our world fell apart,
He was praying,
pouring out his soul to God,
and as I listened my spirit soared,
for it seemed as though our hopes
were about to be realised
and our fears prove unfounded –
that instead of sorrow and death
there would be a happy ending,
our Lord recognised by all,
acclaimed and worshipped,
enthroned in glory.
He spoke of authority from God,
of fulfilling the mission he'd been sent to achieve,
so I put two and two together and made five,
assuming he expected the dawn of God's kingdom
here on earth
and deliverance at last for his people.
I was right in a way, of course,
for he achieved precisely that,
but he did so through a cross rather than crown,
through apparent defeat
rather than trumpeted victory,
and at first we just couldn't see it.
Had I been in his shoes
I'd have prayed very differently,
begging God to provide another way,
less costly,
undemanding –
but I'd misread things completely,
for his entreaties were for *our* welfare
rather than his own,
for all who would come after him,
for the world itself.
That's what mattered most, even at such a time,
not *his* fate but *ours* –

that we should share his joy,
his life,
his kingdom,
now and for all eternity.

Silence

Prayer Lord Jesus Christ,
we marvel at the extent of your love,
at the fact that,
in life and in death,
your thoughts were all for *us*
and none for *you*.
We rejoice in your gift of life –
abundant,
eternal,
overflowing –
won for us by your selfless devotion to our cause;
your willingness to suffer in body, mind and spirit,
surrendering all.
Though we will never approach such commitment,
help us, in turn,
to put the welfare of others before our own,
denying ourselves for their sake and for yours.
Amen.

Hymn A new commandment

Comment It's not easy, is it, when our expectations are suddenly and completely overturned; when we're expecting one outcome of events only for them to work out altogether differently? That's what the apostles and followers of Jesus had to come to terms with in the week leading up to the cross. They'd accompanied him into Jerusalem as he was ardently welcomed as the son of David come to claim his throne, and many of them, even at that late stage, probably still hoped he was going to establish some sort of rule and kingdom on earth. Yet, as his words had already repeatedly made clear, this was no ordinary king, his kingdom not of this world.

Music *Take my life, Lord (Fire of Love)* Margaret Rizza

Reading Matthew 25:31–46

Meditation of Simon the zealot

Hang on,
this doesn't make sense,
for he was talking about a *king* just now,
the Son of Man enthroned in glory,
only suddenly he's become the poor,
the homeless,
the hungry –
not just one of the weak
but the lowest of the low.
What's going on?
Did I miss something?
Or did he mean what he said?
He can't do, surely,
for they're poles apart,
couldn't be more different,
yet somehow,
strangely,
he claims they're the same.
He wants us to *serve* –
I get that –
it's what rulers expect.
Only usually that means serving *them,*
not *others*.
Yet Jesus is asking for both,
suggesting you can't have one without the other,
almost as if he doesn't just *care* about us,
but actually *feels* our pain,
our need,
our sorrow.
You'd almost think, to hear him talk,
that *he's* the servant,
ready to stand in our place,
suffer what's rightly ours,
but that's ridiculous, of course,
for what sort of king would do that?
No, he must mean something else,
but I can't imagine what.
Can *you*?

Silence

Prayer Saviour Christ,
help us to worship you as King of kings
yet servant of all;
as Lord of lords,
yet broken on a cross;
as lifted high,
yet brought low;
as the giver of life,
yet enduring death.
Teach us what your way involves,
your kingdom means,
your victory cost,
and grant us the humility and love we need in turn
to be ready to serve rather than be served.
Help us to walk your way of unassuming commitment,
faithful to the end.
Amen.

Hymn Amazing grace

Comment It's impossible for us to read about Judas Iscariot with an open mind. Our perspective is inevitably coloured by the knowledge that he betrayed Jesus, handing him over to his enemies with a kiss in Gethsemane. But, of course, his fellow apostles were not to know that until the moment it happened. Beforehand, he was simply one of their number, to their mind no doubt sharing their hopes and fears, confidence and confusion. Only through grasping that truth can we begin to understand the shock and bewilderment they must have felt as the events of his betrayal unfolded.

Music *Miserere nobis (Awakening in Love)* Margaret Rizza

Reading John 13:21–32

Meditation of Judas Iscariot

They looked at me mystified,
wondering where on earth I was off to,
what business I could have at such a time of night.
An errand, they assumed,
some mission for the Master,
much as when he'd sent some of the others off
to prepare the upper room
or fetch that donkey from Jerusalem.
They suspected nothing, even then –
never dreamt treachery was afoot
despite all he'd said about death and betrayal.
Gullible fools!
Not Jesus, though –
he knew the score.
And I realised, with a sudden chill,
that he'd understood all along what I was going to do,
not simply when I hatched the plan
but earlier still,
before it even entered my head.
He knew the sort of man I am –
the weaknesses deep within,
temptations I fall prey to –
and he recognised that when the chips were down,
I'd sell out to the highest bidder,
take the cash and run.
Why did he call me, I wonder, knowing that truth?
Why did he welcome me as a disciple and friend?
Yet he not only did that,
but, unless I'm much mistaken, he *loved* me too,
actually cared about my welfare
even as I walked out of that door into the darkness.
I'd expected anger, reproach, disappointment,
but there was nothing of that in the look he gave me –
only compassion, concern, even sympathy.
It was as though he was ready for the end –
that, foolish as it may seem,
he was willing to die not just for his friends
but for his enemies,
not just for others,
but for *me*!

Silence

Prayer Lord Jesus Christ,
teach us more about the way you walked;
the path of love, service, mercy and compassion.
Remind us of your openness to all;
your willingness to give and go on giving.
Remind us of your humility;
the way you invariably put others before yourself.
Help us to understand how much you surrendered,
how much you cared and continue to care,
and may that knowledge inspire us in turn
to consecrate our lives to your kingdom,
seeking always and in everything
to know and do your will.
Amen.

Hymn Jesus the Lord said: 'I am the Bread'

Comment If there's one thing we admire it's those who practise what they preach, and nowhere do we see that better than in Jesus. 'I give you a new commandment,' he said: 'that you love one another' (John 13:34a), and as the opening verse of John 13 reminds us, he loved his own to the end, surrendering everything for their sake. Who are 'his own'? The apostles? The Church? A select few? No, it's *all* of us – you, me, everyone! As we prepare to break bread and share wine together, we remember the one who, in walking the way of the cross, didn't just talk of love but showed us what it means.

Music *The blessing-cup (In God Alone)* Andrew Moore

Reading John 13:1–17a, 31b–35

Meditation of Peter What would you have done in his shoes,
knowing your back would be cut to ribbons,
your head punctured by a crown of thorns,
your hands and feet nailed to a cross?
Would you have gone calmly to your fate,
willingly accepted the torment of skin stretching,
muscles tearing,
organs failing,

as you writhed in agony,
life ebbing all too slowly away?
You'd endure it, of course, if you had to –
yelling, gasping, cursing,
you'd somehow get through.
But if there was some way –
any way –
of avoiding it, you'd take it, wouldn't you?
Grab it, more like, with both hands.
And if anyone could have done that, it was Jesus.
He could have walked away,
stepped down from the cross,
taken a different course –
anything being possible for him –
but,
amazingly,
incredibly,
he *didn't,*
choosing instead to take what they threw at him,
to endure sorrow, suffering, darkness and death.
Why, you ask?
One reason, pure and simple:
for people like you and me.
He loved every one of us, as we are –
not just in life,
but also in death –
his love unlike any other,
reaching out now and always,
to the very end.

Silence

Prayer Gracious Lord,
thank you for what you were willing to go through
for our sakes –
everything you endured
to redeem and restore the world.
Thank you for facing sorrow to bring us joy,
darkness to bring us light,
suffering to bring us healing,
death to bring us life.
Help us to give a little back to you

who gave so much for all.
Amen.

The Eucharist

Hymn Broken for me, broken for you

Closing prayer We acknowledged our emptiness, Lord,
and you made us full.
We recognised our thirst,
and you satisfied our need.
We confessed our faults,
and you granted us pardon.
We declared our weakness,
and you gave us strength.
We consecrated our brokenness,
and you brought us healing.
We mourned our inability to change,
and you made us new.
For the wonder of what you have done
and all you have given,
we praise you.
Amen.

Maundy Thursday (2)

Suggested visual material

Jesus of Nazareth 5
The Life of Christ III
Bread and Wine
Oberammergau 1990
Man of the Cross
He Carries our Cross

Introduction

'This is my body, broken for you . . . my blood, shed for you . . . Do this in remembrance of me' – words of Jesus to his disciples that have been repeated across the centuries in countless observances of the Lord's Supper. And Maundy Thursday, of all days, reminds us just what it is we remember and celebrate, focused as it is on that last meal Jesus shared with his intimate circle before going out to face his death. It reminds us of how, betrayed, denied, abandoned, still he stayed true to his path; of how he wrestled with fear and doubt in Gethsemane; of how he knelt to wash his disciples' feet – Lord, yet servant of all; of how he faced the darkness of death to bring light to the world. And we rejoice in his promise that one day we will break bread and share wine again, with him and all his people, in his Father's kingdom. In this service, then, let us once more remember, and give thanks.

Opening prayer

Gracious God,
nothing we can do,
nothing we can say,
can ever thank you enough
for what you have done in Christ –
for your great love made flesh through him.
As we remember, once more,
his anguish in Gethsemane,
his sacrifice for those who would fail him,
his faithfulness to the last,
we marvel,
awed and humbled by his selfless devotion,
his offering himself for us all.

Help us, today and every day,
whenever we share this meal,
to do so not as a matter of routine,
the observance of a traditional ritual,
but with a sense of wonder and privilege,
recognising what you endured.
what you achieved
and what you promise,
through him.
Amen.

Hymn From heaven you came

Comment We're so used to hearing the words 'My body, broken for you' in relation to bread at the Lord's Supper that we barely bat an eyelid. We know what it means, what it refers to, and it doesn't strike us as in any way strange. But, according to John's Gospel, Jesus first made the association not as he shared bread and wine with the apostles, but after he had fed the multitude with loaves and fishes, going on afterwards to speak of eating the flesh of the Son of Man and drinking his blood; strange words indeed. For those listening to him at the time, with no indication on the horizon of his suffering and death, such words must have seemed hugely puzzling. No wonder some were confused! Yet what he gives here to those willing to listen is an in-depth explanation of this simple celebration; his offering through his death of bread of life to us all.

Music *And with his stripes we are healed (Messiah)* Handel

Reading John 6:51–58

Meditation of one of the crowd listening to Jesus

This has gone from bad to worse!
It's not just weird,
but gross,
grotesque,
for he's talking of giving us his flesh,
of his body being living bread that all must eat.
What does he think we are?
Cannibals!

He's got us not just puzzled but angry,
arguing bitterly over his words.
And can you blame us?
Oh, I've tried to make sense of them,
to see them in a different light,
but what else can he mean?
It seems more than plain.
Even his supporters are struggling with the idea,
some siding openly with his enemies,
and it's no surprise,
for what sane person wouldn't draw the line
at such strange teaching?
It's caused confusion and offence as nothing before.
He's got to be careful, Jesus,
if he doesn't want to meet a sticky end,
for the mood's turning ugly,
many who once followed him
starting to feel that enough's enough.
And though the Pharisees have backed off so far,
afraid of sparking riots,
if the crowds abandon him, he'll be sunk.
Mark my words,
there'll be no mercy.
Blood will be spilt,
his body broken,
his flesh pierced and torn.
Doesn't he know that?
He must do,
for whatever else, he's no fool,
yet he carries on regardless.
Well, let him talk of giving life to the world
if he wants to;
it will end with him giving *up* his life . . .
and what will he achieve by that?

Silence

Prayer Lord Jesus Christ,
thank you for willingly being broken to make us whole,
for enduring death to bring us life.
Thank you for seeing our emptiness
and offering food for the soul,
for understanding our hunger deep within
and providing eternal nourishment,
sufficient for all our needs.
Teach us to recognise all you gave,
all you so readily sacrificed,
and to marvel afresh at the extent of your love.
In faith, may we eat of your living bread,
and be truly satisfied.
Amen.

Hymn Bread of heaven, on thee we feed

Comment Reading a story that we know well is never quite the same as reading it for the first time, simply because we know what's going to happen. So, with the Last Supper, when Jesus says 'one of you will betray me', we understand full well who he means, and are waiting for Judas to get up and do the deed. But, of course, the disciples didn't know the story, for they were part of events as they unfolded, so the effect of Jesus' words must have been profound. Did they already have their doubts about Judas? Or did they simply look around in confusion, suddenly unsure of anyone, anything, including themselves?

Music *Miserere mei* Allegri

Reading John 13:21–32

Meditation of the Apostle John We didn't have a clue,
not the first idea what was going on.
so we looked around in utter confusion.
What could he mean: one of us would betray him?
We were his friends,
devoted and loyal to a man,
or so at least we'd thought,
but it was scary how quickly that belief changed.

Suddenly we doubted each other,
our expressions a mixture of guilt and accusation,
eyes studiously averted from too long a gaze.
I could tell that some even wondered about me,
and why not,
for clearly our assessment of character
was not as good as we'd liked to think.
Even after Judas got up and went out,
having taken that piece of bread,
we still didn't get it,
assuming instead he'd business to attend to.
But Jesus knew what he was up to,
as he'd no doubt known all along.
What, then, of you and me?
Does he know what *we're* thinking too,
what's going on deep inside?
I rather think he may do,
and that's disconcerting, to put it mildly,
for there's so much I'd rather keep hidden,
firmly under wraps.
Would he still have time for me if he knew the worst?
Would he still welcome me as a follower
if he saw who I really am?
I'd think twice in his shoes, that's for sure.
But I tell you what,
when Jesus dipped that bread into the dish
and gave it to Judas,
there was no anger in his eyes,
no disgust or rejection.
Quite the opposite.
It was as though he cared for him as much as ever,
as though he valued him still as a friend.
Could that be true?
Could Jesus have died not only *because* of Judas,
but *for* him, as well?

Silence

Prayer Almighty God,
thank you for the love you have shown in Christ –
a love that sees us as we are,
with all our weaknesses and faults,
and goes on caring;
that knows the worst about us,
coming up against rejection, denial and betrayal,
yet goes on accepting us,
faithful to the last.
Thank you that your grace is not dependent
on anything we might do,
but rests solely with you,
your nature being always to have mercy –
to forgive and restore.
With grateful hearts, we give you our praise.
Amen.

Hymn Overwhelmed by love

Comment A re-enactment of Jesus washing his disciples' feet is now part of many Maundy Thursday services, but what does it mean? It feels thoroughly alien to our modern culture, yet in the time of Jesus it was customary for guests – arriving weary and footsore after walking the dusty roads of Judea – to have their feet washed. The job, though, would be done by a servant, for it was a menial task. In stooping to wash his disciples' feet Jesus was graphically illustrating his way of humility, of serving others, of putting self second and them first – a way he was to demonstrate more powerfully still as he went afterwards to the cross.

Music *Ave Verum* Mozart

Reading John 13:1–17, 31b–35

Meditation of Peter I nearly refused, you know,
the idea of Jesus washing *my* feet
instead of *me, his*
seeming all wrong,
but when he looked me in the eye,

insisting it be done,
I soon changed my tune.
He was the boss after all,
and if that's what he wanted,
that's what he'd get.
In fact I went further,
suggesting he wash my hands and head as well,
for I yearned to walk his way,
and share in his kingdom –
to be made truly clean.
He laughed then,
saying there was no need.
But would he have said the same later,
after I fled from his side
and denied even knowing him?
Nothing after that, I felt, could wash away the dirt
and shame,
but I was wrong,
for through his death on the cross he did exactly that,
bearing the guilt that was mine.
He made me clean –
my feet,
my hands,
my head,
my all –
and if that can be true for such as me,
it's surely so for you.

Silence

Act of foot-washing

Silence

Prayer Lord Jesus Christ,
make us clean, we pray;
wash and make us new.
We are unworthy of your love,
so much in our lives contrary to what you seek.
We are weak and foolish,
our thoughts impure,
our deeds self-centred.

Forgetful of you, we disobey your commandments,
flout your will
and ignore your guidance.
Have mercy upon us, and, by your grace,
cleanse, redeem, restore.
Amen.

Hymn Jesu, Jesu, fill us with your love

Comment Gethsemane will forever be associated with the anguish of Jesus as he wrestled with the prospect of suffering that lay before him, and we should never overestimate quite what he went through at that time. As the following reading and meditation remind us, no other event demonstrates quite so dramatically or movingly that he was human just as we are, vulnerable to the same doubts, fears, sorrow and pain that we endure. Remember what he faced, what it cost him to stay true, and give thanks that he had the faith and courage to do so.

Music *Chanson Triste* Tchaikovsky

Reading John 12:20–36

Meditation of the Apostle James

He was in anguish,
agonising as I'd never expected.
Gone was the inner calm we knew so well,
the tranquillity of spirit we'd come to take as read.
He was trembling,
hurting,
struggling.
We assumed, at first, he was simply scared –
after all, *we* were,
for his enemies were out to get him,
the net closing in.
But there was more to it than that.
He *was* scared, of course,
the thought of what he must go through
filling him with dread,
and if there had been an alternative,

some way of avoiding the agony that lay ahead,
naturally he'd have taken it.
Yet that only made his torment worse,
for he knew also that to be true to himself
and to God
he had to face the future in all its awfulness.
It was his destiny,
the reason he'd come into the world –
to die that we might live –
and what troubled him most
was the possibility of failing in that call.
He *could* have done, you know.
He could have walked away,
saved his own skin,
and no one would have blamed him,
least of all me.
But he didn't;
he trusted instead that God would see him through.
The way ahead was hard,
too dreadful to contemplate,
yet he took it,
in fear and trembling accepting the way of the cross.
Never underestimate what it cost him.

Silence

Prayer Lord Jesus Christ,
too easily we forget what you went through,
what you suffered for our sake.
We focus on your victory over darkness and death,
and overlook the immense price you paid to secure it.
Remind us that your fear was as real
as any we experience,
your pain as intense,
your sorrow as overwhelming,
your torment as acute.
Help us always to remember that, for you,
the cross was no charade,
no play-acting with a guaranteed happy ending;
that, rather, it was an awesome act of faith,
the most powerful demonstration of love and courage
anyone could ever show.

For that great truth,
thank you.
Amen.

The Eucharist

Hymn An upper room did our Lord prepare

Closing prayer Lord Jesus Christ,
bruised and broken,
make us whole.
Gracious Christ,
poured out for many,
fill our hearts.
Vulnerable Christ,
trembling in Gethsemane,
strengthen us in time of need.
Crucified Christ,
hanging in agony,
support those who suffer.
Redeemer Christ,
bearing our sins on the cross,
have mercy upon us.
Saviour Christ,
dying to bring us life,
gladly we receive and rejoice.
Amen.

Maundy Thursday (3)

Suggested visual material

Jesus of Nazareth 5
The Life of Christ III
Bread and Wine
Oberammergau 1990
Man of the Cross
He Carries our Cross

Introduction

Today is a time to remember: to recall the last meal shared by Jesus with his disciples before he faced the agony of the cross, the darkness of death. Today is a time to rejoice: to celebrate the forgiveness, new beginnings and eternal life he makes possible for us all through that supreme sacrifice. Today is a time to look forward in hope: to put our trust in the blessings God holds in store for us and all his people as we share with Christ in his Father's kingdom. Thankful for what he has done, rejoicing in what he is doing and assured of what he will yet do, let us come now in fellowship with him and one another, offering our heartfelt worship.

Prayer

Almighty God,
remind us again today
of the enormity of your love in Christ –
of the extent of his commitment,
the magnitude of his sacrifice,
the depth of his love
and the breadth of his mercy.
Speak to us of his call to discipleship,
his promise of peace,
his healing touch
and his gift of life.
Assure us of his constant presence,
his renewing power,
his compassion for all
and his eternal purpose.
As we consider again his selfless service,
help us to commit ourselves more fully
to the work of his kingdom

and, through him, to offer you now our grateful praise,
in his name.
Amen.

Hymn Lord Jesus Christ

Comment For our first reading and meditation we turn, not to the end of Jesus' ministry, but to the beginning and the wedding feast at Cana. It's an event that at first sight seems far removed from the anguish and sorrow of Holy Week, for surely this was a time of joy and celebration, Jesus contributing to the party atmosphere as he turned water into wine. Yet even then, for those with eyes to see and ears to hear, there were pointers to what lay in store; to the wine that would be poured out for many so that, in time, we may drink new wine with him and all his people in his Father's kingdom.

Music *He turned the water into wine* (*The Gospel Road)*
Johnny Cash

Reading John 2:1–11

Meditation of Mary, mother of Jesus

It seemed a strange thing to say:
'My hour has not yet come.'
After all, I'd only casually mentioned
that they had no more wine.
So what did he mean, I wonder,
by that peculiar response of his?
Not that I let it worry me.
I knew my boy well enough to be sure he'd offer help,
for he never could see someone in need
and pass them by.
Sure enough, he came to the rescue,
producing not just fresh supplies for the party
but the best yet,
special enough for the most discerning palate.
I *should* have worried, though,
and *would* have done, had I understood better,
for this was just a foretaste of things to come;
that hour Jesus spoke of calling, in time,
for new wine of a different sort:

his blood shed for many,
poured out for the forgiveness of sins,
spilled on the cross as he suffered and died for all.
Truly, indeed, the best was saved till last,
the water of the Law and prophets transformed
into the fruit of the true vine,
but at what cost,
what sacrifice,
what sorrow!
Back there, in Cana, that was all in the future,
unknown to all but him,
so we ate, drank and made merry.
He alone knew what was coming,
the awful price he'd be asked to pay
that we might feast with him in heaven.
He saw our need,
he knew what he must do,
and, once again, he couldn't say no.

Silence

Prayer Forgive us, Lord,
for too often we say no to others
and no to you.
We see situations of need around us,
but we hold back,
whether through apathy,
selfishness
or fear of getting involved.
Remind us of what you endured,
what you sacrificed,
to transform our broken world,
and give us faith, love and commitment
to, in some small way, respond in turn.
Amen.

Hymn Let us break bread together on our knees

Comment Holy Week speaks of what Jesus gave for us – of his love, courage, suffering and death – but it speaks also *to* us, asking what we are ready to give in return. What is our response to his sacrifice? What can we do to show our gratitude? How can we demonstrate our love for him? Our next reading and meditation remind us of an impulsive gesture through which one of his followers attempted to answer that question for themselves.

Music *All we like sheep have gone astray (Messiah)* Handel

Reading John 12:1–8

Meditation of Judas Iscariot

All right, so my motives were mixed,
more about my pockets than the needs of the poor,
but I had a point, didn't I?
Give me *that*.
That perfume of Mary's, remember, was expensive stuff:
not just the price of a couple of days' wages
but something you'd have to save up for over weeks,
even months.
Think of the difference the money could have made
to people's lives –
the food it could have put on someone's table,
clothes on a child's back –
and there she was,
pouring it out in one sentimental gesture,
the whole lot wasted in an instant.
It was criminal,
profligate –
that's how I saw it,
and if *she* saw no better use for it,
then, believe me, *I did*!
But far from reprimanding her, as I expected,
Jesus turned on me
as though *I* were the one in the wrong.
What was up with him?
Didn't he care about the poor?
Of course he did, more than anyone,
but he understood, even if no one else did –
myself included –
that to help them, to help *anyone*,

he had first to face death –
and Mary, even if unwittingly,
was anointing his body for burial,
brought about *my* hand.
He cared all right,
as I came finally, but too late, to realise,
not just for the poor but for everyone,
even as lousy a wretch as me –
enough to give his all
to make real change possible in our broken world.
The question is:
do we really care in turn?
And for all my protestations,
all my seeming concern,
the sad truth is that,
to my shame,
I *didn't*.

Silence

Prayer Loving Lord,
teach us to give generously,
to others and to you;
to use the resources you put at our disposal
in your service,
striving in some small way to build a better world,
bringing your kingdom closer here on earth.
Help us to love you more truly
and to show that love through worship and service,
reaching out where we can to those in need.
Through responding to them
may we respond also to you.
Amen.

Hymn Said Judas to Mary now what will you do

Comment Of all the Gospels, John has least to say about the human side of Jesus. He is presented rather as the one who shows us the face of God, who is in control, who walks almost imperturbably towards the cross from the very start of his ministry. So when we read, as we shall in a moment, that Jesus was 'deeply troubled' we sit up and take notice, for, given the context, this is surprising stuff. Suddenly, as he faced betrayal, suffering and death, Jesus was going through the mill, wrestling with hurt, fear, doubt, worry – a whole gamut of emotions each of us will know only too well. Few things remind us more eloquently of the God who shared our humanity, and knows our pain.

Music *Silent, surrendered (Fountain of Life)* Margaret Rizza

Reading John 13:21–32

Meditation of Philip

It was the first time we'd seen him like that –
deeply and desperately troubled.
He'd seemed serene until then,
talking about death as though it were nothing,
so we'd taken his words with a pinch of salt,
assuming he was talking in riddles.
Suddenly though it was all too real,
his face more eloquent than words,
and we realised that all those years we'd known him
he'd lived with the knowledge of what lay in store:
the horror of the cross.
He didn't want to die,
any more than you would,
least of all in such a way,
the thought of the pain he'd endure
filling him with dread.
Yet it wasn't *that* which troubled him most;
it was the risk of failing God,
of fear deflecting him from his chosen path.
It didn't, of course, –
he stayed faithful to the end –
but it was no foregone conclusion,
no inevitable result.
He was troubled,
tormented by doubt and fear,
but one thing swung the balance:
if *his* future mattered to him,
ours did more.

Silence

Prayer

Lord Jesus Christ,
we mean to serve you,
to walk your way,
but we are torn by conflicting desires,
finding it so hard to say yes to you
and no to self.
The spirit is willing but the flesh is weak,
our loyalty stretched to breaking point
when commitment proves costly.
Thank you that your love is different,
putting *us* first and *self* second;
that though the fear, pain and sorrow you faced
were all too real,
your love was more real still,
strong enough to endure the cross
and win us life.
Amen.

Hymn

Love is his word

Comment

Increasingly, today, a Maundy Thursday service includes a reminder of a different sort of service: that which Jesus demonstrated through washing his disciples' feet, and which we, following his example of humility, seek to offer to Christ and one another. But have we understood what serving means? Have we truly grappled with the topsy-turvy values of his kingdom? As our next reading and meditation reminds us, Jesus here, as in so much, was standing the values and expectations of our world on their head.

Music

He was despised and rejected (Messiah) Handel

Reading

John 13:1–17, 31b–35

Meditation of Peter

Would *you* have washed my feet?
I wouldn't have done, in his place,
for they were dirty,
sweaty,
smelly,
so when Jesus approached with that bowl and towel,
well, there's no other word for it,

I was mortified!
He was the teacher,
I the pupil;
he the Lord,
me a mere disciple,
so what was he thinking of,
demeaning himself like that,
as though I were the master
and he the slave!
He was right though:
I *did* understand later,
after they'd whipped him,
struck him,
abused him,
killed him,
everything becoming clear.
Finally, *finally*, it got through to me:
that the last will be first and the least greatest;
that those who lose their life will find it;
that the humble will be lifted up
and the proud brought low.
I needed to learn those values of his kingdom,
so different,
so contrary to our own,
and that night,
as he stooped before me,
was another lesson in love.
He humbled himself,
in life and in death.
a servant to us all.
Will you serve *him* in turn?

Silence

Act of foot-washing

Silence

Prayer In a self-serving world, Lord,
where greed rules,
profit is everything
and looking after number one
is the all-consuming creed,
teach us your way:
the way of humility, sacrifice and service.
Give us the love and courage we need
not just to learn of it
but to put it into practice;
to take up our cross
and follow you.
Amen.

The Eucharist

Hymn Jesu, Jesu, fill us with your love

Closing prayer Lord Jesus Christ,
bruised for our iniquities,
heal our wounds.
Lord Jesus Christ,
broken for all,
nourish our faith.
Lord Jesus Christ,
poured out for many,
refresh our hearts.
Lord Jesus Christ,
betrayed and denied,
assure us of your constant love
though we prove false and faithless.
Lord Jesus Christ,
abandoned in your time of need,
reach out to the lonely.
Lord Jesus Christ,
falsely accused and convicted,
bring justice to our world.
Lord Jesus Christ,
given over to death,
help us to walk in newness of life,
this day and always.
Amen.

Good Friday

Good Friday (1)

(Given that this service traditionally involves time devoted to quiet reflection, I've not included a comment before readings and meditations, allowing these instead to speak for themselves. Whether or not you include audiovisual material is up to you.)

Suggested visual material

Jesus of Nazareth 5
The Life of Christ III
Oberammergau 1990
Man of the Cross
He Carries our Cross

Introduction

Why are we here? To dwell in morbid fascination on the sufferings and death of Christ, the agony he went through in body, mind and spirit? No, though of course as we read once more of that awesome sacrifice we will undoubtedly marvel at his willingness to endure so much for our sakes. So why *are* we here? To focus on sin and weakness, brooding over how unworthy we are to receive God's pardon? Again, and emphatically, no! A preoccupation with our faults, still less an obsession with guilt, has no place in the message of the gospel. No, we are here today to *celebrate*, to give thanks for a love that gave and goes on giving, for a saviour who was broken to make us whole, for a Lord who died to bring us life. This is *Good* Friday, a day of *good news*! Let us rejoice.

Opening prayer

Redeemer Christ,
we remember that you suffered on the cross,
enduring agony of body, mind and spirit,
and entering into the darkness of death,
but too often we forget what that means,
what it actually cost you
and what it makes possible for us.
We have heard the message so many times
that it washes over us,

no longer moving, challenging and inspiring
in the way it once did.
We accept with our heads but not in our hearts,
the sense of awe and wonder
that once burned within us
too easily becoming a spluttering flame,
all but extinguished.
Speak to us again of the immensity of your sacrifice,
the astonishing breadth of your love
and the costliness of your gift.
Help us to stand in spirit at the foot of the cross,
and to marvel afresh at your saving grace,
responding in joyful praise and glad thanksgiving.
Amen.

Hymn There is a green hill far away

Music (optional) *The blessing-cup (In God Alone)* Andrew Moore

Reading John 13:1–17, 31b–35

Meditation of Peter

What would you have done in his shoes,
knowing your back would be cut to ribbons,
your head punctured by a crown of thorns,
your hands and feet nailed to a cross?
Would you have gone calmly to your fate,
willingly accepted the torment of skin stretching,
muscles tearing,
organs failing,
as you writhed in agony,
life ebbing all too slowly away?
You'd endure it, of course, if you had to –
yelling, gasping, cursing,
you'd somehow get through,
but if there was some way –
any way –
of avoiding it, you'd take it, wouldn't you?
Grab it, more like, with both hands.
And if anyone could have done that, it was Jesus.
He could have walked away,
stepped down from the cross,
taken a different course –

anything possible for him –
but,
amazingly,
incredibly,
he *didn't*,
choosing instead to take what they threw at him,
to endure sorrow, suffering, darkness and death.
Why, you ask?
One reason, pure and simple:
for people like you and me.
He loved every one of us, as we are –
not just in life,
but also in death –
his love unlike any other,
reaching out now and always,
to the very end.

Silence

Prayer Gracious Lord,
thank you for what you were willing to go through
for our sakes –
everything you endured
to redeem and restore the world.
Thank you for facing sorrow to bring us joy,
darkness to bring us light,
suffering to bring us healing,
death to bring us life.
Help us to give a little back to you
who gave so much for all.
Amen.

Hymn Beneath the cross of Jesus

Music (optional) *On the holy cross I see (Music for Lent, Holy Week and Easter)* Keith Duke

Reading John 18:1–19:42

Meditation of a soldier at the foot of the cross

We watched him die,
stood there, as we'd stood for so many others,
while he squirmed in agony,
grimaced with pain.
It was nothing new to us,
just another day's work,
the gasps and groans of our victims,
their tortured screams and sobs,
falling on deaf ears.
Yet somehow, from the start, this man was different,
meeting everything we threw at him –
the crown of thorns,
the flogging,
the nails hammered through hands and feet –
with awesome dignity and courage.
It got under our skin,
stirring a voice of conscience long since suppressed,
for it was obvious to everyone,
even the most jaundiced among us,
that he was innocent of any crime,
his punishment undeserved.
Oh it happens, I know that,
many a luckless wretch sharing the same fate
through no fault of their own,
but usually they scream their innocence,
beg for mercy,
rail against the injustice of it all.
Not Jesus, though.
He suffered all right,
as much as the next man,
but somehow he seemed in control,
not just of himself
but of *everything*,
almost as if he'd *chosen* to hang there –
as though he believed his death, however unmerited,
was able to achieve something,
to serve a greater good.
'It is finished!' he cried eventually,
and in his eyes we saw not defeat,
as you might have expected,
but triumph,
a look of joy that spoke of mission accomplished,

job done.
I still can't work it out, even now,
but I'm resolved to try,
for I tell you this:
we didn't *take* his life that day;
odd though that may sound,
he gave it!

Silence

Prayer

Saviour Christ,
we thank you for going to the cross,
knowingly,
purposely,
lovingly,
your death being not an awful accident
or tragic mistake,
but a supreme expression of your love.
We praise you for being not only ready to die
but *resolved* to do so,
committing yourself,
from the beginning of your ministry,
to surrender your life in order to redeem the world.
Teach us to live each day
in the knowledge of how much we matter to you,
and to celebrate the new beginnings you offer to all.
Amen.

Hymn When I survey the wondrous cross

Music (optional) *Requiem (Requiem)* Verdi

Reading Matthew 27:57–66

Meditation of Joseph of Arimathea

I should have done more, I know that,
my feeble gift of a tomb too little, too late.
I should have responded when I could –
declared my love, my loyalty, while he was still alive,
while it might have been put to good use.
But I didn't, did I?
Fear won the day instead.
You can sympathise, surely?

My fellow Pharisees loathed Jesus, remember,
so to be even seen with him,
let alone counted a supporter,
spelt trouble with a capital 'T':
rejection at the least,
more likely a fate such as his.
So what changed, you ask?
What made me,
having kept quiet for so long,
come forward at last,
risking everything for a man who was dead and gone?
Yet that's just it, you see.
He didn't *need* to die,
not if he didn't want to,
for God was with him like no other,
but he offered his life willingly,
in selfless sacrifice,
convinced it would change the world for ever.
I don't know how,
I don't know why,
but I *do* know this:
that no one could have loved me more
or given so much,
so freely.
How could I not respond?

Silence

Prayer Redeemer Christ,
we know we can never thank you enough
for what you have done,
never praise you sufficiently
for the immensity of your grace
and depth of your love,
but save us from using that as an excuse
for failing to honour you as we should.
Help us to show our gratitude
through the people we are:
through hearts open to you,
minds seeking you,
words proclaiming you
and actions serving you.

Small though it may be,
help us to do what we can to honour your name
and to further your kingdom –
truly and lovingly, to respond.
Amen.

Hymn We sing the praise of him who died

Music (optional) *Stabat Mater (Stabat Mater)* Vivaldi

Reading Luke 2:33–35; John 19:25–27

Meditation of Mary, mother of Jesus

We'd laid him in a manger when he was born –
can you believe that!
Not a comfortable cradle, lovingly prepared,
but an animal feeding trough,
a rough-hewn box where cattle had munched
just moments before.
We did our best to make it safe, of course,
laying down a bed of straw
and wrapping him in swaddling clothes
to protect him from the worst,
but we were concerned, nonetheless,
terrified that a splinter might pierce his tender skin,
even perhaps a nail.
It didn't happen, thankfully,
the little mite seeming quite content . . .
and eventually we relaxed
enough to enjoy the moment.
But it was only a reprieve,
for, when he became a man,
my son was to be pierced after all,
by both splinters *and* nails,
great lumps of metal hammered through his hands
and feet,
crushing bone,
tearing sinew,
before they lifted him on to a cross,
and greedily watched him die.
'Why didn't he come down?' I asked myself.
He could have done, I knew it.
Why hadn't he whipped up the crowds

while he had the chance,
mustered them to his side so that,
by sheer weight of numbers,
he'd have been safe from his enemies,
at least for a time?
He could have called down bolts from heaven,
routed the opposition,
made a bid for the throne,
but he didn't do any of those,
and, deep down, I *knew* the reason why,
for it wasn't the rewards of this world
that interested him,
but the *people* –
ordinary people like you and I –
our welfare,
our future,
our fate.
He could have saved himself;
he chose instead to save others.
He could have clung on to life;
he chose to *give* it instead.
His sole concern was to deliver from evil,
to rescue and redeem,
and as, through the tears, I watched him die,
I realised as never before that,
however much we'd treasured that bundle in the hay,
however much we'd longed to keep him safe,
he cared, and continues to care,
a thousand times more –
for us
and for all.

Silence

Prayer

Gracious God,
for being willing to surrender your beloved Son,
your one and only child,
we praise you.
For caring about *us*
with the same intensity as you cared about *him*,
the same passion and devotion,
we worship you.
For inviting us to be your children,
as special and precious to you
as any child is to its mother,
we thank you.
Speak to us of how deeply you value us,
how much it cost you to make us your own,
and help us to respond with heartfelt homage
and joyful commitment.
Amen.

Hymn

From heaven you came

Closing prayer

Send us out, Lord,
rejoicing in your love,
renewed by your grace,
challenged by your word
and inspired by your sacrifice.
Equip us to speak *of* you,
point *to* you,
work *for* you,
live *through* you.
Go with us
and, in all we do, help us to seek your truth,
show your compassion,
celebrate your blessings
and strive for your kingdom.
Amen.

Good Friday (2)

(Given that this service traditionally involves time devoted to quiet reflection, I've not included a comment before readings and meditations, allowing these instead to speak for themselves. Whether or not you include audiovisual material is up to you.)

Suggested visual material

Jesus of Nazareth 5
The Life of Christ III
Oberammergau 1990
Man of the Cross
He Carries our Cross

Introduction

From 'Hosanna!' to 'Crucify!' From 'the King of Israel!' to 'We have no king but Caesar!' There, in miniature, is not just the backdrop to Good Friday but the rationale behind the cross, the reason Jesus had to suffer and die. For in that stark about-turn, that abrupt shift from welcome to rejection, we see the human condition writ large. The shouts of praise as Jesus entered Jerusalem had been real enough, but they had rested on a misunderstanding of who Jesus was and what he came to do. Even the disciples, when the moment came, were found wanting, failing to grasp the truth. 'He was in the world, and the world came into being through him; yet the world did not know him. He came to what was his own, and his own people did not accept him. But to all who received him, who believed in his name, he gave power to become children of God, who were born, not of blood or of the will of the flesh or of the will of man, but of God' (John 1:10–13). That's why Jesus went to the cross: to do what we could never do alone, to make possible what we could never deserve. Today, as we reflect again on the immensity of his love and extent of his sacrifice, let us marvel afresh at the debt we owe and the gift we have received through him.

Opening prayer

Loving God,
we come to worship,
to rejoice,
to give thanks –
to remember that,
in Christ,
you endured the darkness of sorrow,
suffering
and death
in order to bring us light.
We come seeking pardon and new beginnings,
not because we have any claim on your blessing,
but trusting solely in your grace,
in your love which,
while we were yet sinners,
freely gave all.
Weak,
foolish,
unworthy though we may be,
take what we are
and direct what we shall become,
through Jesus Christ our Lord.
Amen.

Hymn Who can sound the depths of sorrow

Music (optional) *Rex tremendae (Requiem)* Verdi

Reading John 18:33–37

Meditation of Pontius Pilate

He was putting words into my mouth,
and must have known it,
for I'd offered a question,
not a statement.
It was *him* claiming to be a king,
or so his enemies said,
and, much as I wanted to,
I couldn't just ignore it,
for any talk like that,
from the Jews especially,
spelt trouble.
They'd rebelled before, remember,

and felt the full weight of our displeasure as a result,
so the last thing any of us wanted
was some misguided pretender
stirring up a hornets' nest once more.
Yet the strange thing is, he *wasn't* pretending,
of that I'm sure.
He knew, quite clearly, both who he was
and what he was doing,
there being an unnerving assurance about him,
an inner integrity,
that nothing could shake.
Believe me, I tried to break him,
but it couldn't be done,
for he bore whatever we threw at him
with quiet dignity,
even that crown of thorns pressed on to his head –
almost as if he were *glad* to wear it,
as if such suffering said it all.
I was baffled by the man,
troubled,
for though I held his fate in my hands,
he seemed to think otherwise –
seriously imagining that, beaten and broken,
he could yet be Lord of all.
I should have discounted the idea, I know that,
but I couldn't,
for such was his extraordinary demeanour
that part of me feared he was right.
He'd got under my skin,
so I vainly attempted to offer him life,
but he chose death instead,
as though somehow that could offer more.
Ridiculous, isn't it,
for what kind of king takes his throne
through a cross?
Yet strangely,
disturbingly,
though *I* put the question,
I couldn't help feeling it was *he* who asked it.

Silence

Prayer

Lord Jesus Christ,
teach us the way of your kingdom,
so that we may understand what it means
to honour you.
Teach us that you reign on high,
not because you seized a crown,
but because you endured a cross;
not because you considered equality with God
something to be grasped,
but because you emptied yourself,
taking the form of a servant,
and humbling yourself to the point of death.
Help us to recognise that your kingship runs contrary
to the way of the world,
turning so many of our values and expectations
upside down,
your rule being through consent rather than coercion,
lovingly offered rather than forced upon us.
Saviour Christ,
King of kings and Lord of lords,
we address you as such –
help us to mean it.
Amen.

Hymn O dearest Lord, thy sacred head

Music (optional) *Behold the Lamb of God (Messiah)* Handel

Reading John 19:1–16

Meditation of Pontius Pilate

I tried to save him, give me that.
Okay, so I caved in eventually,
but wouldn't you have done the same in my shoes?
I'm answerable to Caesar, remember,
and if he thought, even for a moment,
that I'd let him down,
sanctioned what might be construed as treason,
then it would have been *me* facing death,
never mind Jesus.
Not that he was guilty –
any fool could see through that –
but for some reason his accusers despised him,

refusing to back down until he was sealed in a tomb.
I did everything I could to change their minds –
offered to release him,
tried to compromise,
gave chance after chance for them to think again –
but they wouldn't listen,
and neither would *he*!
In all honesty, what could I do?
Yet, despite my efforts, I still feel bad,
not just because he was so clearly innocent,
but because there was something about him
that shook my confidence,
leaving *me*, the most powerful man in Jerusalem,
feeling powerless,
as though *I* – the one hearing his case –
was being tried.
I should have made a stand,
set him free and faced the consequences,
for in failing to be *for* him,
I was *against*.
I realise now that you can't wash your hands
of some decisions,
however much you try.
You must choose between good and evil,
right and wrong –
for taking no decision is a decision in itself.
He offered forgiveness, so they tell me,
as he hung from his cross.
Can you believe that!
Well I hope he includes *me* in that pardon,
for though I pretend otherwise,
I've no excuse for what I did . . .
and what I failed to do.
Jesus, if it's not too late,
believe me, I'm sorry.

Silence

Prayer Lord Jesus Christ,
we mean to stay true to you,
to stand up for what we believe,
but time and again, when put to the test,

we sit on the fence,
reluctant to commit ourselves,
afraid of the consequences.
We come up with excuses to justify our actions,
with reasons for what we do and fail to do,
but the reality is we put self first and you second,
our own interests before those of your kingdom.
Forgive us,
and give us deeper faith,
greater courage,
truer commitment.
Have mercy,
for we are truly sorry.
Amen.

Hymn O sacred head, surrounded

Music (optional) *Ave Maria* Schubert

Reading Luke 2:33–35; John 19:25–27

Meditation of Mary, mother of Jesus

We'd done our best for him,
packing straw into the manger
to make it as soft and safe as possible.
But if I thought I could protect Jesus from danger,
such confidence was swiftly to be questioned,
those words of Simeon's
about a sword piercing my soul
sending a chill up my spine.
And, as if to reinforce the threat,
soon afterwards we had to rush off to Egypt,
in fear for our lives from Herod.
Afterwards though, I dared to dream again,
for we enjoyed happy years together in Nazareth,
just another family quietly going about our business.
I still worried of course –
mums always do, don't they?
but it was only after he began preaching and teaching,
healing the sick,
restoring the broken,
proclaiming the kingdom of God,
that my fears resurfaced.

Many followed him,
loving Jesus just as I did,
but inevitably he ruffled feathers,
plenty not liking what they heard.
He challenged so much they held dear,
not just questioning the status quo
but threatening to sweep it away altogether.
No surprise, then,
that the scribes and Pharisees resolved to silence him,
and eventually seized their chance.
I watched bereft as they nailed him to that cross;
blood seeping from his head, his hands and his feet.
And as he hung there,
convulsed by the pain,
I shared his agony,
my heart broken as only a mother's can be.
I wanted to reach out to hold, protect and comfort.
And when he finally spoke,
entrusting me into the care of his most trusted friend,
I realised he wanted to do precisely the same for me.
I held a special place in his heart,
understandably,
but I'm not the only one.
You do, too,
every one of you.
In the awfulness of his suffering,
his concern was still to love –
to bring healing through his brokenness,
life through his death.
I'd done my best for him;
now he was doing *his* best,
not just for me,
but for all.

Silence

Prayer Lord Jesus Christ,
thank you that though we deserve it so little
you love us so much;
that you value each of us infinitely,
enough to die for.
Thank you for staying true to your chosen path,

despite the hostility you faced,
the misunderstanding you endured,
the pain you suffered
and the darkness you confronted.
In the ugliness that scars the beauty of this world,
the shadow of evil, hatred and death,
teach us that your light shines through
and your love will triumph,
life, now and for all eternity,
being held safely in your hands.
Amen.

Hymn Mary, blessed grieving mother

Music (optional) *He trusted in God (Messiah)* Handel

Reading Matthew 27:57–66

Meditation of the chief priest

It's sorted at last, thank God!
That Jesus fellow silenced for good.
Heaven knows what might have happened
had we failed to act,
There would have been hell to pay, mark my words.
You should have seen the crowds that followed him,
heard the things they said.
The Messiah, they shouted,
the son of David,
the one sent to set us free.
We've had enough pretenders already,
thank you very much,
and look where they got us:
hopes raised only to be dashed,
followed by brutal and bloody reprisals.
So, you see, we had to stop him,
and we did,
though that weasel Pilate made things harder
than they needed to be.
At least he's come up with what we need now –
a guard of soldiers to watch the tomb –
for he knows as well as any
that we can't afford the body to go missing
and his disciples spinning some cock-and-bull yarn

about him being alive after all.
No, he's dead all right –
we stayed to the end to make sure of that –
and his body was cold when we sealed it in the tomb.
There's a boulder against it now,
and it would take an army to shift it,
so even his most devoted followers
will have to accept that it's over,
finished,
time to go home.
Jesus is staying put, right where he is,
unless, of course, he can defeat death itself,
and somehow I don't think *that's* likely.
Do you?

Silence

Prayer Sovereign God,
thank you that when evil had done its worst,
when darkness seemed victorious
and death to hold sway,
you were supremely at work.
Thank you that,
though hatred appeared to have crushed love
and truth to have been destroyed by falsehood,
even and especially there
you were working out your purpose.
Thank you that every effort to thwart your will
was futile;
that nothing and no one could conceal the triumph
you won for us in Christ.
Whatever we face,
in life or in death,
teach us that nothing will ever separate us
from your love in him.
Amen.

Hymn Come and see

Closing prayer

Lord Jesus Christ,
you were acquainted with grief –
help us to weep over what destroys and denies life.
You were silent before your accusers –
help us to speak for you.
You faced up to darkness –
help us to shed your light.
You took on the forces of evil –
help us to work for good.
You wiped the slate clean –
help us to start again.
You gave your all –
help us to give something back.
You *died* for us –
help us to *live* for you.
Amen.

Good Friday (3)

(Given that this service traditionally involves time devoted to quiet reflection, I've not included a comment before readings and meditations, allowing these instead to speak for themselves. Whether or not you include audiovisual material is up to you.)

Suggested visual material

Jesus of Nazareth 5
The Life of Christ III
Oberammergau 1990
Man of the Cross
He Carries our Cross

Introduction

This is the darkest of days yet the brightest: a day when we remember a cry of despair yet also a shout of triumph; when we're reminded of the starkness of evil but also the power of love. It speaks of sorrow but also of celebration, of abject betrayal yet equally of awesome faith; of an immeasurable cost asked and an awesome price paid. That is the mystery of this day – one that we can truly call *Good* Friday, for though it recalls the very worst of moments it recalls also the very best: a day that changed the world!

Opening prayer

Sovereign God,
we marvel at the extent of your love,
at how much you were willing to sacrifice
for our sake.
We remember how you surrendered your only Son,
through him enduring hostility,
rejection,
sorrow
and suffering –
bearing the awful burden of human sinfulness,
and nailing it to a cross.
For that stunning grace –
willing to accept the punishment
that was rightly ours,
giving your life that we might truly live –

joyfully we praise you.
Help us, today, to recognise afresh
the wonder of the cross;
to grasp not just with our minds but in our hearts
the full meaning of what you have done
and continue to do;
so that we may worship you now
and honour you always,
through Jesus Christ our Lord.
Amen.

Hymn It is a thing most wonderful

Music (optional) *Surely he hath borne our griefs (Messiah)* Handel

Reading John 19:1–16

Meditation of Pontius Pilate

I could find no case against him,
no charge to answer.
He wasn't a rebel, urging revolt,
nor some usurper with designs on power –
his intentions, in terms of this world,
were clearly harmless, albeit misguided.
He'd hurt no one,
wronged no one,
yet clearly he'd caused offence,
for those infernal scribes and Pharisees.
with their never-ending rules and regulations,
wanted him dealt with:
not just punished or imprisoned,
but dead.
That wouldn't have bothered me in the usual run –
what's one less troublemaker? –
but this Jesus fellow unnerved me from the start.
Those eyes of his!
Those quiet yet assured replies!
They threw me completely,
seeming to say *my* fate was in *his* hands,
rather than *his* in *mine*.
Where was he from, I wondered?
Who could he be?
A visitor from the gods?

And as that alarming thought took hold,
I tried to set him free.
But it was hopeless,
the pack having scented the kill,
and the harder I pleaded his cause
the louder they bayed for blood.
I gave in, eventually.
What choice did I have?
Rather his neck on the line than mine.
But I've not slept easy since,
that gentle innocent face of his haunting my dreams .
I found no case against him,
yet sent him to his death,
and I'm just hoping now
that he's not who he claimed to be –
king of another world –
for, if he was,
I fear one day another verdict may be delivered . . .
in a case against *me*.

Silence

Prayer Suffering saviour,
for receiving the sentence that is ours,
facing the punishment that is ours,
bearing the sin that is ours,
enduring the death that is ours,
we worship you.
Receive the thanks, praise, worship and service
that is rightfully yours,
and, in your mercy,
help us to celebrate the victory you have won
and to walk each day in newness of life,
cleansed,
renewed,
forgiven.
Amen.

Hymn My song is love unknown

Music (optional) *Rex tremendae (Requiem)* Mozart

Reading Luke 23:33–43

Meditation of one of the soldiers who crucified Jesus

What was all that king stuff about?
He didn't look very regal to me,
stuck up there on the cross,
a crown of thorns thrust on his head.
Yet there it was,
writ large above him:
'This is the king of the Jews'.
A sick joke, we decided,
Pilate's way of showing that troublesome people
just who was boss.
And good thing too,
for they were always up to something,
determined to hassle us if they could.
Yet this time, strangely, they were jeering *him*,
not *us*,
cursing and shouting insults at that Jesus fellow
worse even than ours.
Whatever throne he laid claim to,
they didn't recognise it,
all of them apparently, save the merest handful,
resolved to see him go.
So we joined in the fun,
delighted for once to have the mob on our side.
Only, now, I wish we hadn't,
for there was something strange about the way
he hung there,
the way he suffered and died.
None of your usual anger or self-pity.
No cries for mercy or oaths of vengeance.
Just an uncanny, awesome dignity
even as he shuddered in agony . . .
and when he spoke,
it was with words of forgiveness,
love,
almost, it seemed, a hint of triumph,
as though, despite *us* having put him there,
he was in control.
He'd saved others, so some said –
why didn't he save himself?
But then, what would a true king have put first:

his throne,
or his subjects?
It made me wonder, I don't mind admitting it –
perhaps, after all, he *was* a king.
Quite how, I can't fathom,
but I tell you what,
if it was meant as a joke calling him 'king of the Jews',
it badly backfired that day,
for in some strange, but unmistakable way,
he had the last laugh.

Silence

Prayer Lord of lords and King of kings,
teach us to honour you
through living by the values of your kingdom:
to serve you through *serving*,
love you through *loving*,
give to you through *giving*.
Come into our hearts,
our lives,
our world,
and rule among us.
Amen.

Hymn You laid aside your majesty

Music (optional) *Ave Maria* Gounod

Reading Luke 2:33–35; John 19:25–27

Meditation of Mary, mother of Jesus I was so proud,
so happy as I held our child close,
cradling him in my arms.
He seemed more special,
more precious,
than I'd dreamt possible,
and I wept tears of joy.
But just days later,
a shadow fell that was never quite to lift,
for that man Simeon, as we took Jesus to the Temple,
warned of hurt,

heartbreak,
a sword piercing my soul.
And now, all this time later,
after years of wondering,
hoping he might be wrong,
I've come, all too clearly, to see what he meant.
For it's my boy up there, hanging on that cross;
it's my boy, grimacing with pain;
it's my boy, broken and bleeding;
it's my boy, breathing his last –
and no words can express my pain.
He brought it on himself, in a sense,
choosing the way of the cross,
and though I'd begged him to think again,
I'd known all along, in my heart of hearts,
that there was no other way –
that he had to fulfil his calling.
My heart ached with pride,
even while it groaned with grief,
and, if earlier, joy had been touched with sorrow,
now sorrow was touched with joy,
for as he writhed there in agony,
he looked down at me
and showed how much he cared,
asking John,
his dearest, closest friend,
to look after me –
treat me like a mum.
I had to let go of my child –
we all do, don't we? –
his life having brought me both pleasure and pain,
laughter and tears.
But, whatever the cost, it was worth it,
a thousand times over,
for through him, I've been truly blessed,
and so also, if you've only eyes to see it, have *you*.

Silence

Prayer For the wonder of your love, Lord,
poured out for many;
for the immensity of your sacrifice,

offered for all;
for the depth of your care,
never exhausted;
for the richness of your blessing,
so freely given;
from the bottom of our hearts, we thank you.
Amen.

Hymn Were you there when they crucified my Lord?

Music (optional) *Lacrymosa dies illa (Requiem)* Mozart

Reading Matthew 27:57–66

Meditation of Mary Magdalene

We sat there, stupefied,
too numb to cry,
too shocked to take it in –
to accept that our friend,
our teacher,
our Lord,
was dead.
But he *was*.
We'd watched it all,
the whole terrible nightmare
unfolding before our eyes.
We'd seen the crown of thorns pierce his head,
the soldiers strike him across the face,
the whip lacerate his flesh
and the spear thrust into his side.
We'd heard the groans,
the gasps,
as they hammered in nails,
as they hoisted up the cross,
as he hung there in agony,
limbs outstretched,
muscles tearing from bone.
And, finally, that last defiant shout
as he bowed his head
and gave up his spirit.
There was no denying it,
much though we longed to.
He was dead,

his broken body cut down
and sealed in a tomb.
Our hopes were dashed,
our master gone –
our world, it seemed, was over.

Silence

Prayer Remind us, Lord, that you are there
even in the darkest moments of life:
moments of hurt and betrayal,
of crushing disappointment,
of pain and sorrow,
of death itself, in all its apparent finality.
Remind us that, whatever we face,
you have been there before us,
to prepare the way
and see us through.
Amen.

Hymn Lord, there are times

Closing prayer Lord Jesus Christ,
you love us so much:
help us to love you better.
You surrendered all:
help us more truly to serve you.
You walked the way of the cross:
help us to carry ours in turn.
You died to set us free,
help us live in newness of life.
Instead of being forgotten when we leave this place,
put aside for another year,
may the message we have heard again today
shape the way we think,
the words we say,
the deeds we do
and the people we are.
Help us to give something back to you
who gave so much for us.
Amen.

Easter

Easter (1)

Suggested visual material
Jesus of Nazareth 6
The Life of Christ IV

Introduction

After night comes morning; after rain, sunshine; after tears, laughter; after endings, new beginnings. That is the message of Easter, the good news at the heart of our faith. Christ has died. Christ has risen! After defeat came victory. After the cross, the empty tomb. This is the day that changes every day, the beginning that makes all things new. Let us relive the experience of those who met the risen Lord face to face, and let us walk and talk with him in turn, sharing their joy and wonder. Together let us rejoice in the resurrection life that shapes life itself!

Opening prayer

Into the darkness of our world,
your resurrection brought light.
Lord, we rejoice.

Into the despair of our world,
your resurrection brought hope.
Lord, we rejoice.

Into the emptiness of our world,
your resurrection brought purpose.
Lord, we rejoice.

Into the enslavement of our world,
your resurrection brought liberty.
Lord, we rejoice.

Into the sorrow of our world,
your resurrection brought joy.
Lord, we rejoice.

Into the brokenness of our world,
your resurrection brought healing.
Lord, we rejoice.

Love conquered hatred,
good, evil,
and death, life.
Lord, we rejoice.
Amen.

Hymn Christ is risen! Alleluia!

Comment To realise just how good life is we need to understand how bad it can be. To appreciate our many blessings we need to consider those less fortunate than ourselves. So often the reality of a situation only fully comes out in contrast to another, and so it is supremely with Easter, as we will explore again in this service. Take first the two Marys as they made their way to the tomb. Were they struck, I wonder, by the brightness of the new dawn after the long night hours, by the radiance of morning light breaking into the darkness? Probably they were too overcome with grief to give such things a moment's thought. But there was another new dawn, another light shining in the darkness, that they soon couldn't possibly miss, for the stone was rolled away and the tomb empty. Death had given way to life, endings to new beginnings! That is the truth of Easter both then and now – for the women, for the apostles, and for all. Whoever you are, whatever life may bring, never lose sight of the fresh start God offers you in Christ.

Music *Laudate Dominum (Music for Lent, Holy Week and Easter)* Margaret Rizza

Reading Matthew 28:1–10

Meditation of the other Mary

It was a bolt from the blue . . .
literally . . .
shattering the peace of the garden
and breaking in rudely on our grief.
We'd walked there in silence,
each wrapped up in our thoughts,
remembering all the special things

Jesus had said and done,
precious moments neither of us would ever forget
but that had been so cruelly snatched from us
as they nailed him to a cross.
Both of us were fighting back the tears,
struggling to be strong for the sake of the other,
but as we approached the tomb
we could feel ourselves crumbling,
great sobs welling up within,
and we'd have caved in completely
had it not been for that astonishing turn of events.
Suddenly,
without any warning,
any clue as to what was about to happen,
the ground seemed to shake and lightning fill the sky,
as though heaven itself was breaking in upon us,
and so, of course, it was to prove,
in a way more wonderful
than we could have dared imagine.
In that awesome, earth-shattering moment,
God was at work,
transforming the world for ever;
not only us but everyone,
not only life but death.
For Jesus had risen,
victorious over evil,
triumphant over the grave.
The tomb was empty,
and he was alive once more,
waiting to meet and greet us,
to speak his word again and walk with us on the way.
And this time, whatever might be,
there would be no separating us from his love,
no tearing us apart –
for we knew that, through his Spirit,
he would be with us always, to the very end of time.

Silence

Prayer Almighty God,
we remember with awe the first Easter morning,
marvelling that, at a time when you seemed absent,
you were supremely at work,
and at a place where death seemed triumphant,
new life was coming to birth.
Remind us, should we ever forget,
that you are a God of surprises,
a God who turns the expectations of this world
upside down,
bringing hope out of despair,
laughter out of tears,
light out of darkness
and life out of death.
In that knowledge,
may we never despair of any situation,
no matter how bleak or hopeless things may seem.
Help us always to keep faith
in your transforming power –
able to make us and all things new.
Amen.

Hymn Alleluia, alleluia, give thanks to the risen Lord

Comment For Mary Magdalene, the significance of the empty tomb was slow to register. She saw for herself that the body of Jesus was no longer there, but instead of hope this simply brought added despair, the suspicion that someone had sneaked in during the night and taken the corpse away, adding insult to injury. So it was that she wandered aimlessly around the garden, eyes blinded by tears, her world – so she imagined – broken beyond repair. Not even Jesus by her side could at first break through her misery, until slowly the truth dawned: the stranger, whom she took to be a gardener, was none other than her Lord and Master himself. Then, after sorrow came joy, after tears laughter. Life is turned around – ours as well as hers – for though it brings grief hard to bear it promises also, by God's grace, to yield joy that will never end.

Music *I know that my redeemer liveth (Messiah)* Handel

Reading John 20:1–18

Meditation of Mary Magdalene

I was distraught,
eyes blinded by grief,
heart numb with sorrow,
for I honestly believed they'd taken away his body
and I'd never see Jesus again.
All right, he was dead,
so what does it matter, you say?
But it did to me,
for I wanted to pay my respects,
to gaze on that gentle face,
that lovely man,
just one more time.
I wanted to remember him at peace,
not groaning on a cross;
to see him laid to rest
and know his suffering was truly over.
And now, it seemed, I was to be denied even that,
his corpse stolen like some grisly trophy,
pursued to the last by his enemies.
It all but finished me,
and I broke down in tears,
conscious of nothing and no one but my grief.
Not even those strangers in the tomb
could shake me from it –
my only thought being
that someone had taken away my Lord,
and I'd no idea where they'd laid him.
No point looking, I thought –
he was gone,
lost to us for ever.
But I was wrong –
wonderfully, gloriously wrong –
for I'd no need to find him at all:
he found *me*!

Silence

Prayer Risen Lord,
with hearts ablaze,
filled with praise and wonder,
we celebrate the truth that death is not the end;
that you rose from the grave,
opening the way to life for all.
With a song on our lips,
heartfelt hymns of joy and thanksgiving,
we celebrate the fact that love is stronger than hatred,
good greater than evil,
and light mightier than darkness.
With laughter in our eyes,
sparkling with faith and hope,
we celebrate the proof that sorrow will turn to joy,
hurt to wholeness
and defeat to victory.
With gratitude deep within,
filling body, mind and spirit,
we celebrate the assurance
that your kingdom will never end,
your purpose never fail
your love never fade
and your mercy never be exhausted.
Gladly, we worship you.
Amen.

Hymn This is the day, this is the day

Comment Few Easter stories are more familiar than that of Thomas, and few also seem to speak so emphatically of contrasts, in this case between faith and doubt. Yet are things as straightforward here as they seem? Would the other apostles have reacted any differently in Thomas' place? When Jesus first appeared before them, did they at first believe what their eyes were telling them? An unbiased look at the Easter narratives suggests they did not. The fact is that they struggled to take in the wonder of the resurrection, just as we do, because it runs contrary to everything the world tells us. We want to accept it, yes, but is it too good to be true? Are we simply clutching at straws, naively indulging in wishful thinking? Many will accuse us of just that – of swallowing an empty delusion – but despite hostility, ridicule, persecution and controversy, generations across the centuries have continued to trust, their personal experience conquering inner doubts. That's what happened for Thomas, his meeting with the risen Christ dispelling his questions and inspiring him to kneel instead in grateful worship. For us, too, such a meeting is the answer to our prayer: 'Lord, I believe; help with my unbelief.'

Music Sanctus *(Requiem)* Verdi

Reading John 20:19–31

Meditation of Matthew

I feel sorry for Thomas,
for people talk of him in the same breath as doubt,
as if the two are synonymous,
each belonging together.
Okay, so he didn't believe at first, I'll grant you that,
but he wasn't alone:
we *all* struggled at the beginning
to accept it was really him –
our friend Jesus, returned to life
and standing there among us.
We'd seen him crucified, remember,
his body dragged from the cross and laid in a tomb,
limp and lifeless.
And when we'd gathered together
that first day of the week,
the doors were locked and bolted,
for we were petrified our enemies would come for us
as they'd come just days before for Jesus.
Would you have expected him to stroll in suddenly
as if nothing had happened?
To appear out of the blue by your side,
alive and well?
Of course not.
You'd have pinched yourself, as *we* did,
rubbed your eyes in amazement
convinced you were seeing things,
the light playing tricks with your eyes.
Not one of us believed completely

until he showed us his hands and side;
and we could see for ourselves it was true.
So don't be too hard on Thomas . . .
or on yourself,
for Jesus didn't condemn him
any more than the rest of us.
He asks for faith,
and he'll help it to grow,
but he also understands doubt,
and will help that to *go*.

Silence

Prayer Loving God,
when we find faith hard,
all kinds of questions forcing themselves
into our minds,
all sorts of doubts arising unbidden
and refusing to be quelled,
save us from hiding them away,
as if they are a guilty secret,
a weakness to be ashamed of;
and save us from pretending they aren't there –
sweeping them under the carpet
and struggling on with them unresolved.
Teach us to bring them honestly before you,
seeking your guidance and insight,
so that we may understand more of you
and your ways.
Nurture our belief,
and help us to deal with our unbelief,
through Jesus Christ our Lord.
Amen.

Hymn Jesus lives! Your terrors now

Comment 'We're on a road to nowhere,' sang the group *Talking Heads* in the 1980s, but such words could just as easily have been sung by the two followers of Jesus walking the Emmaus Road, for that's precisely how they must have felt. They wouldn't have done so a week earlier, for they'd made their way then to Jerusalem full of hope and expectation, no doubt convinced like the rest of the disciples that the kingdom of God was upon them; that the man they'd followed with such fervent devotion was about to take up his throne and rule among them. How differently, though, things had turned out, Jesus not being crowned but crucified. And with his death everything that they'd believed in, worked towards and longed for seemed to have been snatched from their grasp for ever. What could the future hold now, for them or anyone? What meaning could there be in life when God had seemingly abandoned them in their time of need. No doubt they put such questions to the stranger who joined them on the road, so strangely unaware of the awful events that had so recently unfolded. It was only when they broke bread together that the penny dropped and their world lurched on its orbit once again. They were on the right road after all, not just to Emmaus but to the kingdom of heaven. They were on a journey of discipleship, a call to follow the way of Christ – a pilgrimage we are called to share, travelling each day in the light of Easter faith.

Music *Irish blessing (Sacred Weave)* Keith Duke

Reading Luke 24:13–35

Meditation of Cleopas

We were returning to Emmaus,
heading back the way we'd come,
but in truth we were going nowhere,
life suddenly empty,
devoid of direction,
for they'd crucified Jesus,
the one on whom we'd pinned our hopes.
We'd thought him the Messiah,
the promised one of God who'd set us free,
and when he'd ridden into Jerusalem
acclaimed like a king
we'd assumed the time had come,
the moment when he'd take up his throne
and start to rule.
But now he was dead,
and with him had gone our faith in the future,

our faith in *anything*.
What sort of God would let that happen?
Why hadn't he intervened?
We tried to make sense of it as we talked together,
but there too we trod the same old ground –
one step forward and the next backwards.
Until, that is, this stranger met us
and walked by our side.
Until we broke bread and shared wine.
Until he opened the Scriptures
and unfolded their meaning.
Then, suddenly, we knew the truth.
It was Jesus –
risen,
victorious,
alive!
That's why God let it happen.
He *had* intervened, right there on the cross!
And though Jesus vanished even as the truth dawned,
we knew somehow he'd be with us always,
the King of kings and Lord of lords.
We set off again,
resuming our journey,
but this time we were no longer going nowhere:
we were walking the way of Christ!

Silence

Prayer Risen Lord,
remind us that, with you by our sides,
faith should be an ongoing journey,
an unfolding story of adventure and discovery.
Give us an expectation of new experiences and insights,
an openness to new horizons,
a desire to grow in grace, wisdom and commitment.
Reveal your presence to us through your word,
your world,
your Church,
your Spirit,
and help us to greet each day in the knowledge
that you are with us,
leading us forward,

whatever we face,
in life or in death –
each moment being another step on the road
to the joys you hold in store,
now and for evermore.
Amen.

Hymn Thine be the glory!

Closing prayer Risen Lord,
fill us with eternal life –
free,
abundant,
overflowing.
Put new faith in our hearts,
new love in our eyes,
new fire in our bellies,
your resurrection shaping everything we think,
say
and do.
Take what we are
and transform what we shall be,
through your sovereign power.
Amen.

Easter (2)

Suggested visual material

Jesus of Nazareth 6
The Life of Christ IV

Introduction

A day that changed history – such a claim has been made in relation to numerous occasions across the years, with varied justification. A good number, no doubt, have powerfully shaped people's lives, for better or worse, but none will have had the far-reaching influence of the event we recall today, or the same capacity to change lives for ever. Why? Because we do not simply celebrate the resurrection of Jesus, astonishing though that may be. We rejoice rather in the defeat of death itself, in Christ's victory over the grave, his triumph over everything that denies, demeans and destroys life. That's what Easter is about: life for you, for me, for all; life lived now in a new dimension, transformed by his touch; life for eternity. In our service today we reflect on that glorious truth; on what it means to proclaim 'Christ is risen! He is risen indeed!'

Opening prayer

Living God,
with joyful hearts we praise you,
for you have destroyed the power of death
and opened the way to life.
With humble hearts we acclaim you,
for you have vanquished evil,
good refusing to be denied.
With grateful hearts we acknowledge you,
for you have turned defeat into victory,
ends into new beginnings.
With reverent hearts we honour you,
for you have changed our lives for ever,
making this and every day a celebration of Easter.
Living God,
for the triumph you achieved,
and the victory you go on achieving,

we magnify your holy name,
through Jesus Christ our Lord.
Amen.

Hymn Jesus Christ is risen today

Comment For us today, Easter morning is full of hope, a day that speaks of new beginnings, but for the followers of Jesus on that first Easter it was anything but. Jesus was dead and buried, their world had fallen apart, and they were left reeling, broken, devastated. The women who set off at the crack of dawn did so not with any sense of expectation but with heavy hearts, going simply to make their last tearful farewells. Or so at least they thought. What happened next, of course, was to transform their lives in a way they could scarcely have dreamt possible.

Music *Alleluia (Exsultate, Jubilate)* Mozart

Reading Mark 16:1–8

Meditation of Salome

We had our spices ready to anoint his body,
a last gesture of devotion to our Lord,
but, in all honesty,
we thought it would be a wasted journey,
for they'd rolled a mighty stone across the tomb
and set a guard to keep watch.
So why go, you ask?
Why waste our time on a fool's errand?
It's a fair question,
but what else were we to do?
We were numbed by grief, remember,
distraught and wretched beyond words.
And we needed to do something,
anything,
to dull the pain.
More than that, however stupid it may sound,
we wanted to be near Jesus,
dead though he was –
to feel that somehow the bond between us
wasn't entirely broken.

If we could even approach the tomb,
view it from a distance,
it might help a little, we thought.
And who could say,
if the soldiers took pity on us,
perhaps they might even roll the stone away
for a moment,
long enough for us to embalm his body
as we had intended.
So we went,
hoping against hope,
yet not even in our wildest dreams
daring to contemplate what we found
when we got there.
It was a wasted journey all right,
totally so, in one sense,
but not because we couldn't see his body.
Astonishingly,
incredibly,
there was no body to see!
The stone had been rolled away,
the tomb was empty –
Jesus was alive!

Silence

Prayer Gracious God,
again we praise you for the wonder of Easter,
again we rejoice in the good news of Christ –
your victory, through him, over death and evil,
your triumph over darkness and despair,
your defeat of whatever would deny your love
and frustrate your purpose.
For the joy you have brought us –
the assurance of new life, now and for all eternity –
we worship and adore you.
Amen.

Hymn They had lost the will to live

Comment John's Gospel gives us another account of that first Easter morning, capturing once again that mixture of awe, wonder and disbelief that the women must have felt when first confronted with the empty tomb. They'd come thinking it was the end of the story and found instead that a new chapter had only just begun. They'd thought life held nothing, only for it suddenly to promise everything. Imagine how it must have felt.

Music *Hallelujah (Messiah)* Handel

Reading John 20:1–18

Meditation of Mary Magdalene

We thought he'd gone for ever,
that he'd been taken from us never to return,
for we'd seen Jesus breathe his last,
watched as they hauled him from the cross
and laid him in the tomb.
He was dead,
no doubt about it,
and we were all devastated,
overwhelmed by a tide of despair,
like ships at sea without an anchor.
What would have become of us, I wonder?
Perhaps we'd have drifted back to our old way of life,
carried on as best we could,
but I'm not sure we'd have managed it,
for we were broken,
empty,
the void too big to fill.
Thankfully, it didn't come to that,
for when we reached the tomb
we found, not a cold, lifeless corpse,
but the stone rolled away,
the grave clothes lying there, but no body!
He was risen,
alive!
We thought he'd gone,
and so he *had*,
but not as we imagined.
He'd gone *ahead* of us,
a light for our path and lamp to our feet.

He'd faced the darkness of death,
and opened the way to life.
Seen or unseen,
we know now that he's always there,
ahead of us still,
leading us safely forward,
in this world and the next,
to our journey's end.

Silence

Prayer Living God,
we praise you that the gospel speaks
not just of what you've *done,*
but also of what you're *doing,*
not simply of the resurrection of Jesus long ago,
but equally, and all the more so, of his risen life now
and the new life he offers to us in turn.
Thank you for the way, through him,
you are able to transform every moment,
bringing joy out of sorrow and hope out of despair.
And thank you for the knowledge that,
whatever life may bring,
you are with us, through your Spirit,
to lead us forward from darkness into light.
Teach us to put our trust wholly in you,
confident that, come wind or rain,
sunshine or shadow,
you will be there by our side,
now and always.
Amen.

Hymn Jesus, stand among us, in thy risen power

Comment Do you ever have doubts about resurrection? Not that of Jesus, but your own in the fullness of time? We hold on to that promise. We trust in it. And yet we struggle, literally, to put flesh on the bones. What will resurrection life be like? Where will we live it? How can it happen? Questions such as these are hard to avoid and harder still to answer, to the point that many of us on occasions will echo those celebrated words from Mark's Gospel (9:24): 'Lord, I believe. Help my unbelief.' If that's you, then take heart, for you're not alone. As we've noted already, the disciples initially discounted the account of the empty tomb, and Thomas refused to believe that Jesus had appeared to his fellow disciples. Yet their doubts were to be overcome as Jesus met with them and walked and talked by their side, the reality of his living presence instilling a sure and certain faith in his resurrection power that could not be shaken.

Music *I know that my redeemer liveth (Messiah)* Handel

Reading John 20:19–31

Meditation of Thomas

Did he condemn me for doubting?
Not a bit of it –
he understood,
and answered.
Perhaps I should have believed earlier –
after all, I had my fellow disciples' word
that Jesus was alive –
but you can appreciate I wanted to be sure.
Don't forget, we were grief-stricken when he died,
numb with despair,
none of us listening when Mary and the others
rushed back from the tomb
declaring it was empty and the Lord raised –
no, not one.
We feared it was wishful thinking,
a beautiful but sad delusion,
for though Jesus had spoken of rising again,
we never imagined it could really happen.
It was just my luck not to be there
when he appeared to them all,
and I longed to accept their story afterwards.
Yet I didn't dare to trust,
lest it were all to prove a ghastly mistake.
I couldn't have lived with more disappointment,
not after what we'd been through already,
so I closed my mind to the idea
until Jesus stood before me,
inviting me to touch, and feel, and know.

Seeing is believing,
isn't that what they say,
and so it was for me.
So how, you may ask,
can anyone possibly believe without seeing?
Well actually they *can*,
for even though he's gone from us now,
returned to the Father,
I know he's with me still,
every moment of the day –
here through his Spirit in his risen power.
I can't see him,
but I can feel his presence,
for ever by my side.
Not that you have take my word for it –
I wouldn't expect that.
Respond,
and discover the truth for yourself.
Do not doubt,
but believe!

Silence

Prayer Lord Jesus Christ,
we have faith in you –
in who and what you are,
what you mean,
what you have done
and what you will yet do.
But we also have doubts –
things we don't understand,
that we cannot make sense of,
that we struggle to accept.
Alongside our belief is unbelief,
alongside trust, uncertainty.
Accept us, we pray, despite the warring voices within.
Deepen our faith and respond to our doubts,
assuring us of your living presence and constant love.
Though we will never have *all* the answers,
teach us that, in you,
we have the one answer we really need.
Amen.

Hymn He is Lord

Comment For the followers of Jesus in the days after the resurrection, it wasn't just their Lord who had come alive, it was everything. Life took on a whole new meaning, for from that point on it was lived in the context of eternity. Death had been defeated. Hatred and evil had done its worst and been conquered. Yes, the fulfilment of God's eternal purpose still lay in the future but, in Christ, God's kingdom had dawned and its final victory was assured. What previously had been hidden was now revealed. What had been a mystery now made sense. Through the risen Christ, everything was different.

Music *Spring song in A* Mendelssohn

Reading Luke 24:36b–48

Meditation of Joanna, a companion of the disciples

How did we not see it before?
How could we have missed
what was staring us in the face?
It's a puzzle to me,
to us all,
but that's the way it was.
When they arrested Jesus in the garden,
dragged him before Pilate;
when they nailed him to that cross
and sealed him in a tomb;
we'd believed that was it,
the dream over,
the adventure at an end.
After all, we saw he was dead with our own eyes,
watched him draw his last breath,
so there could be no denying it,
no clutching at straws.
We wanted to, heaven knows!
But what was the point of pretending there was hope,
when it was all too clear there was none.
So we'd simply given in to sorrow,
a paralysing, consuming grief,
and we'd be wrestling with that now,

had nothing changed.
But change it did,
wonderfully,
gloriously –
death defeated,
the Lord risen!
He's been with us again today,
laughing, smiling, eating in our presence,
unmistakably alive,
and as he opened the Scriptures to us,
just as he'd done earlier
for our friends on the Emmaus Road,
the truth suddenly became obvious,
leaping out at us from the page.
It was as he'd said:
the Messiah must suffer
and rise from the dead on the third day –
the empty tomb not the undoing
of some awful catastrophe
but part of God's plan,
the fulfilment of his purpose of old.
We hadn't seen it before,
and no doubt there's much we still don't see,
but we know one thing now for sure:
that he's constantly with us,
leading us to a greater understanding of truth
and richer experience of his love,
each day a new beginning
through his resurrection life.

Silence

Prayer Loving God,
we have begun to understand the miracle of Easter,
but so much escapes us;
we have grasped a little of your resurrection power,
but have far more still to learn.
We read the Scriptures,
but too often we do not see what's there before us.
We declare our faith,
but our commitment is limited.
Open our eyes,

our minds
and our hearts to the living Christ,
so that we may know the truth more fully
and celebrate each day the new life
you have won for us through him.
Amen.

Hymn Alleluia, sing to Jesus

Closing prayer Lord Jesus Christ,
the disciples failed at first to believe in the empty tomb,
dismissing it as so much nonsense,
and we too are hesitant to believe sometimes,
fearful of indulging in wishful thinking,
in what seems too good to be true.
The Apostle Thomas refused to accept
you had truly risen,
insisting he would not accept it
until he could see you for himself,
touch and feel your wounds,
and we too struggle with doubt,
questions to which we cannot find answers.
Your followers on the Emmaus road
and Mary in the garden
failed to recognise you though you stood by their side,
and our eyes too can be closed to your living presence,
here with us now.
Yet you greeted the disciples in the upper room,
you showed yourself to Thomas,
you spoke to Mary
and you made yourself known
through bread and wine.
Across the centuries
you have likewise met with your people,
guiding, nurturing and inspiring through your Spirit.
You have changed history,
changed lives,
changed *us*.
Thank you.
Amen.

Easter (3)

Suggested visual material

Jesus of Nazareth 6
The Life of Christ IV

Introduction

Easter is not just a one-off day each year, to be celebrated and then forgotten. It is a season of celebration balancing the reflective mood of Lent and sombreness of Holy Week. More than that, it is an event providing the context in which we live, its message shaping everything we do and are, to the point that some have suggested that another name for us, apart from Christians, might be 'Easter people'. The empty tomb and risen Christ speak of new beginnings, of a fresh start both now and beyond the grave. Here, if anywhere, is proof that hatred and evil will not have the final word; that sorrow will turn to joy and defeat to victory. Together, let us celebrate the triumph of God's love and the future he holds in store.

Opening prayer

Sovereign God,
we rejoice today in the wonder of this season,
the good news of the resurrection of Christ.
We marvel that you conquered evil
and defeated death.
We give thanks for the new life you have won,
not just for us
but for everyone –
life now in all its fullness,
life eternal, beyond the grave.
Forgive us for failing to believe
as fully as we should.
Forgive us for returning to our old ways,
spurning the fresh start you so freely offer.
Forgive us for forgetting what you are able to achieve
through your mighty strength.
Come now into our hearts and rekindle our faith,
into our world and fulfil your purpose.
Lift us from death to life.
Amen.

Hymn Christ the Lord is risen today

Comment What was the initial response to the resurrection of Jesus? Joy? Praise? Celebration? Laughter? You might have thought so, but the reality is very different. It was scepticism, doubt, disbelief – an inability to accept it could possibly be true. And when you think about it, that's hardly surprising, for although Jesus had spoken to his followers several times about rising from the dead, they'd suffered the trauma of seeing their friend and master nailed to a cross and sealed in a tomb. Which of us after that, any more than they did, would have expected to see him again?

Music *Gloria in excelsis Deo (Gloria)* Vivaldi

Reading Luke 24:1–12

Meditation of Peter

Amazed?
Is that how they tell you I felt?
Well, that's one word for it, I suppose.
I'd put it differently:
astounded,
flabbergasted,
staggered beyond words.
He was dead remember,
his body taken down from the cross
and sealed in a tomb,
and every one of us had been convinced it was over,
our hopes and dreams laid to rest.
Yes, we'd seen him raise others, it's true,
but that was different:
who could raise *him*?
No point pretending, we thought,
our Lord had gone
and we were on our own.
So when the women came back from the garden,
all excitement and confusion,
I was like the others at first,
dismissing their words as idle fantasy.
It was only slowly,
as they pressed their case,

that those words of Jesus came back:
about dying and rising again,
death itself conquered.
Could it be true, I wondered?
Surely not!
And I was torn between a desire to run and see . . .
and to run away.
I chose the first finally,
for I *had* to know,
just in case,
and incredibly it was all just as they had said,
the stone rolled away,
the grave clothes discarded,
the tomb empty.
He'd been dead,
no doubt about that.
But now,
marvellously,
gloriously,
he was alive!
No doubt about that either!

Silence

Prayer Lord, we rejoice in the wonder of this day,
the awesome, amazing truth
that you rose from the tomb,
conquering death and defeating evil.
We celebrate your appearing to your disciples
and your presence with us now –
the way you have walked and talked
with your people across the centuries,
kindling faith,
sharing love
and inspiring service.
Receive our joyful praise for all you have given:
life now
and life to come.
Amen.

Hymn Can it be true, the things they say of you?

Comment Easter, above all, is about Christ's victory over death, but resurrection embraces far more than that, as we see from the experience of the apostles and the story of the early church. As Paul so memorably put it, even though they were dead they were constantly being made alive, renewed in faith, hope and love. Whatever setbacks they faced, whatever defeats they suffered, they bounced back from it, assured of the final victory of Christ. The appearance of Christ to his disciples represented new beginnings in more ways than one.

Music *Alleluia (Exsultate, Jubilate)* Mozart

Reading John 20:19–31

Meditation of the Apostle James

It wasn't just the *doors* that were locked –
it was our hearts as well,
shut tight against the Jews,
the future
and the truth.
We were terrified that the Pharisees would come for us
as they'd come so recently for Jesus;
that they'd do to us what they'd done to him.
We dreaded what lay ahead,
convinced that, without Jesus, we could never cope.
And yes,
though faith should have stirred again within us
after those reports of the empty tomb,
the stone rolled aside,
the Lord risen –
still we couldn't quite accept it,
none of us daring to believe
in case it were some cruel delusion.
So we sat there,
too shocked to face the past,
too shaken to trust the future,
too shattered to live in the present,
each of us imprisoned by fear, grief and doubt.
Until, that is,
as so often before,
Jesus stood among us!
He was alive,

victorious,
by our side once more!
No door could keep him out.
No grave could keep him in.
And suddenly our hearts were open,
set free to live again.
Whatever had been,
whatever was,
whatever would be,
Jesus was there too.
What more did we need to know!

Silence

Prayer Whatever our worries in the present,
whatever our fears for the future,
teach us, Lord, to trust in you,
assured that, in life or in death,
your love is stronger than all.
Help us to live each day,
each moment,
in that sure and certain faith.
Amen.

Hymn Led like a lamb to the slaughter

Comment Think of Easter and we think automatically of what God has done for us, opening the way to everlasting life. But there's another side to this season, relating to what we can do for him. After the risen Christ appeared to his disciples, it wasn't just a question of going back to the way things had been before. The onus subsequently was upon them to go out in his name and to proclaim the news of his resurrection, so that others too might come to see and know him for themselves. That's what we see in our next reading: a call not just to the apostles but equally to us today.

Music *Morning (Peer Gynt)* Grieg

Reading John 21:1–19

Meditation of Nathanael

It was like the loaves and fishes all over again,
only this time there was no multitude to feed –
just us, a handful of disciples.
We'd been fishing all night,
and were famished,
but there seemed no prospect of food,
for, despite all our efforts,
all our skills,
we'd caught nothing.
Only, then, Jesus appeared,
and suddenly everything changed,
our nets,
after we let them down where he told us to,
not just full
but fit to burst.
We'd enough and more than enough,
breakfasting that day like kings!
We trawl for *people* now instead of fish,
but it's the same story,
the same lesson we need to learn.
for if the call is *ours*,
the mission is *his*.
We have a part to play,
but results are down to him.
We can do nothing,
he does all.
Never then think success depends on you –
your words,
your gifts,
your ingenuity –
for you couldn't be more wrong.
Let down your nets –
lovingly,
honestly,
faithfully –
and *he* will supply the catch.

Silence

Prayer In all you call us to do, Lord,
everything you call us to be,
remind us that we do it not in our strength
but through yours.
Teach us that what is impossible for us
is possible for you;
that what we could never hope to achieve
through our own efforts
can be accomplished by your resurrection power.
Help us, then, to work for you,
speak for you,
live for you,
love for you,
confident that if we do our part,
you will do yours.
Amen.

Hymn You stood there on the shoreline

Comment If only we had *proof* of the resurrection, concrete and unassailable evidence that it really happened – wouldn't that be wonderful?! There would be no question then of some believing and others not, nor would there be any controversy about the whys and wherefores of the empty tomb or the nature of eternal life. Everything would be straightforward, faith and new life shared by all. But is it actually that simple? Even if Jesus were to appear large as life in our towns and cities today, would people accept him, believe in him, commit themselves to his cause? The words of our next reading pose a tantalising question: could Jesus ever have proved he was alive again to those who didn't want to believe? And can he any more do so today?

Music *Lift up your heads O ye gates (Messiah)* Handel

Reading John 10:22–30

Meditation of a Sadducee listening to Jesus

Why didn't he tell us who he was?
Why beat about the bush,
talking in parables and riddles,
when he could have made things clear?
Was he the Messiah or wasn't he?
But he wouldn't come clean,
seeming determined instead to keep us guessing.
Well, what could we make of that?
It seemed obvious he wasn't the Messiah after all,
but that he wanted us to think he might be;
that, despite all his claims to the contrary,
he enjoyed the mystique,
the attentions of the crowd,
and wanted to keep it going.
Even then, though, we wanted to believe,
hoping we might be wrong,
so we put him on the spot,
asking him to give it to us straight,
one way or the other.
And what did he talk about in reply?
Sheep!
I know, extraordinary, isn't it.
He seemed to imply we had only to listen
and the truth would be revealed,
but that we'd made up our minds already
and were resolved *not* to hear.
What nonsense!
The truth is that, for all his signs and wonders,
God's reign on earth seemed as far away as ever,
consigned to some future kingdom
rather than established here today.
Well I'm sorry,
but we don't go in for all that pie in the sky nonsense,
resurrection and eternal life,
and we never will
unless someone comes back from the dead to prove it.
Let Jesus do that and we'll revise our opinion,
of him and everything,
for *of course* we'll believe –
who wouldn't? –
but I don't think that's likely.
Do *you*?

Prayer

Living Lord,
in a sceptical and cynical world that refuses to believe,
help us to keep faith in you.
Though we cannot prove you rose again,
or that *we* will either,
may your voice continue to ring true within us,
speaking of your risen presence and promise of life –
a sure and certain hope.
Amen.

Silence

Hymn

Low in the grave he lay

Closing prayer

Living God,
we have met you here –
help us to see you everywhere.
Where lives are broken,
truth is crushed
or justice is denied,
bring new beginnings.
Where hopes are thwarted,
faith is destroyed
or life is ended,
bring resurrection.
Where suffering scars,
sorrow weighs heavy
or hurts are hard to bear,
bring life in all its fullness.
Go with us now into our world of need,
and help us to walk there, through his Spirit,
with the risen Christ.
Amen.

Visual Resources

As indicated in the Foreword, few visual resources that I'm aware of are currently in print, but you should be able to order at least some of those listed below through your local library or diocesan resource centre. As well as the collections mentioned, I have occasionally used slides of the Holy Land, particularly, for example, scenes of the wilderness to accompany meditations on Jesus' temptation or John the Baptist preaching in the desert. It's worth also looking online for other images, such as Davis Art Images (see http://www.davis-art.com/Portal/DAI/SlideSets_Default.aspx?curPage=ProductDetails&ModelNumber=LI FA1; Davis Publications, Inc., 50 Portland Street, Worcester, MA 01608), for portrayals of Jesus in art. For me, still the most powerful visual depiction of Jesus is that in the six-set pack of 144 slides based on the television series *Jesus of Nazareth* directed by Franco Zeffirelli, produced by the Bible Society.

(Note: An asterisk indicates that the resource is no longer commercially available. Those not marked are still in print, as far I know.)

*Jesus of Nazareth 1: Jesus – Birth & Childhood**
*Jesus of Nazareth 2: Jesus – Begins his Ministry**
*Jesus of Nazareth 3: Jesus – Heals**
*Jesus of Nazareth 4: Jesus – Cares**
*Jesus of Nazareth 5: Jesus – In the Last Week**
*Jesus of Nazareth 6: Jesus – Trial to Resurrection**
Colour transparencies from the TV series directed by Franco Zeffirelli. Produced by the Bible Society.

The Life of Christ I (Annunciation, nativity, and childhood)
The Life of Christ II (Christ's public ministry)
The Life of Christ III (The crucifixion)
The Life of Christ IV (The resurrection)
Slides focusing on the life of Jesus, as 'seen through the eyes of the artist', produced by Visual Publications,

The Green, Northleach, Cheltenham, Gloucestershire GL54 3EX.

*Jesus, the Child**
A cartoon slide-set produced in conjunction with a Ladybird Bible Book primarily aimed at children. Was produced by the Scripture Union.

*Come let us adore**
A series of 27 slides on the nativity. Was produced by Audio Visual Productions UK.

*The Parables of Jesus**
A slide-set primarily aimed at children. Was produced by the National Christian Education Council.

Oberammergau 1990
A sequence of 36 slides from the Oberammergau Passion Plays, produced by Huber, Drosselstrabe 7, D-8100 Garmisch-Partenkirchen, Germany.

Man of the Cross
A slide-sound presentation (code 70P326), also available as a set of 15 posters (code 73P262), using a variety of artistic media, including photography, vividly portraying the Way of the Cross. Produced by St Paul MultiMedia Productions, 199 Kensington High Street, London W8 6BA.

*He Carries our Cross**
An audiovisual programme for liturgy, prayer and reflection, including slides of line-sketches, focusing on the events of the Passion under two subsections: (a) Journey to Jerusalem, and (b) Journey to the Cross. Was produced by St Paul Audio Visual Productions.

*Bread and Wine**
Pictures of the elements of the Eucharist, particularly suitable for meditations on the Last Supper. Was produced for the Church Pastoral Aid Society by Falcon Audio Visual Aids.